# CAMBRIDGE LIBRARY COLLECTION

*Books of enduring scholarly value*

## Women's Writing

The later twentieth century saw a huge wave of academic interest in women's writing, which led to the rediscovery of neglected works from a wide range of genres, periods and languages. Many books that were immensely popular and influential in their own day are now studied again, both for their own sake and for what they reveal about the social, political and cultural conditions of their time. A pioneering resource in this area is Orlando: Women's Writing in the British Isles from the Beginnings to the Present (http://orlando.cambridge.org), which provides entries on authors' lives and writing careers, contextual material, timelines, sets of internal links, and bibliographies. Its editors have made a major contribution to the selection of the works reissued in this series within the Cambridge Library Collection, which focuses on non-fiction publications by women on a wide range of subjects from astronomy to biography, music to political economy, and education to prison reform.

## A Book of Sibyls

Anne Thackeray Ritchie (1837–1919) was a writer and the eldest daughter of the novelist W. M. Thackeray. She had a tumultuous childhood: her mother suffered from depression and was eventually committed to a sanatorium, and the family experienced poverty before her father's literary success. Anne was extremely close to her father, who admired her intellect and encouraged her writing. When he died, Anne set up house with her sister Harriet and her brother-in-law, the literary journalist Leslie Stephen. Anne's novels were serialised in the *Cornhill Magazine*, which her father had edited, and their success established her literary reputation. *A Book of Sibyls* is Anne's study of four female writers: the poet Anna Laetitia Barbauld and the novelists Amelia Opie, Maria Edgeworth and Jane Austen. For more information on this author, see http://orlando.cambridge.org/public/svPeople?person_id=ritcan

T0370670

Cambridge University Press has long been a pioneer in the reissuing of out-of-print titles from its own backlist, producing digital reprints of books that are still sought after by scholars and students but could not be reprinted economically using traditional technology. The Cambridge Library Collection extends this activity to a wider range of books which are still of importance to researchers and professionals, either for the source material they contain, or as landmarks in the history of their academic discipline.

Drawing from the world-renowned collections in the Cambridge University Library, and guided by the advice of experts in each subject area, Cambridge University Press is using state-of-the-art scanning machines in its own Printing House to capture the content of each book selected for inclusion. The files are processed to give a consistently clear, crisp image, and the books finished to the high quality standard for which the Press is recognised around the world. The latest print-on-demand technology ensures that the books will remain available indefinitely, and that orders for single or multiple copies can quickly be supplied.

The Cambridge Library Collection will bring back to life books of enduring scholarly value (including out-of-copyright works originally issued by other publishers) across a wide range of disciplines in the humanities and social sciences and in science and technology.

# A Book of Sibyls

*Mrs. Barbauld, Miss Edgeworth,
Mrs Opie, Miss Austen*

ANNE THACKERAY RITCHIE

CAMBRIDGE UNIVERSITY PRESS

Cambridge, New York, Melbourne, Madrid, Cape Town, Singapore,
São Paolo, Delhi, Dubai, Tokyo, Mexico City

Published in the United States of America by Cambridge University Press, New York

www.cambridge.org
Information on this title: www.cambridge.org/9781108021241

© in this compilation Cambridge University Press 2010

This edition first published 1883
This digitally printed version 2010

ISBN 978-1-108-02124-1 Paperback

# A BOOK OF SIBYLS

MRS BARBAULD      MISS EDGEWORTH

MRS OPIE      MISS AUSTEN

BY

## MISS THACKERAY

(MRS RICHMOND RITCHIE)

LONDON

SMITH, ELDER, & CO., 15 WATERLOO PLACE

1883

*[Reprinted from the Cornhill Magazine]*

# PREFACE.

Not long ago, a party of friends were sitting at luncheon in a suburb of London, when one of them happened to make some reference to Maple Grove and Selina, and to ask in what county of England Maple Grove was situated. Everybody immediately had a theory. Only one of the company (a French gentleman, not well acquainted with English) did not recognise the allusion. A lady sitting by the master of the house (she will, I hope, forgive me for quoting her words, for no one else has a better right to speak them) said, 'What a curious sign it is of Jane Austen's increasing popularity! Here are five out of six people sitting round a table, nearly a hundred years after her death, who all recognise at once a chance allusion to an obscure character in one of her books.'

It seemed impossible to leave out Jane Austen's dear household name from a volume which concerned women writing in the early part of this century, and although the essay which is called by her name has already been reprinted, it is added with some alteration in its place with the others.

Putting together this little book has been a great pleasure and interest to the compiler, and she wishes once more to thank those who have so kindly sheltered her during her work, and lent her books and papers and letters concerning the four writers whose works and manner of being she has attempted to describe; and she wishes specially to express her thanks to the Baron and Baroness VON HÜGEL, to the ladies of Miss Edgeworth's family, to Mr. HARRISON, of the London Library, to the Miss REIDS, of Hampstead, to Mrs. FIELD and her daughters, of Squire's Mount, Hampstead, to Lady BUXTON, Mrs. BROOKFIELD, Miss ALDERSON, and Miss SHIRREFF.

# CONTENTS.

# A BOOK OF SIBYLS.

## *MRS. BARBAULD.*

1743–1825.

' I've heard of the lady, and good words went with her name.'
*Measure for Measure.*

### I.

' THE first poetess I can recollect is Mrs. Barbauld, with
whose works I became acquainted—before those of any
other author, male or female—when I was learning to
spell words of one syllable in her story-books for children.'
So says Hazlitt in his lectures on living poets.   He goes
on to call her a very pretty poetess, strewing flowers of
poesy as she goes.

The writer must needs, from the same point of view as
Hazlitt, look upon Mrs. Barbauld with a special interest,
having also first learnt to read out of her little yellow
books, of which the syllables rise up one by one again with
a remembrance of the hand patiently pointing to each in

B

turn ; all this recalled and revived after a lifetime by the
sight of a rusty iron gateway, behind which Mrs. Barbauld
once lived, of some old letters closely covered with a wavery
writing, of a wide prospect that she once delighted to look
upon.    Mrs. Barbauld, who loved to share her pleasures,
used to bring her friends to see the great view from the
Hampstead hill-top, and thus records their impressions :—

'I dragged Mrs. A. up as I did you, my dear, to our
Prospect Walk, from whence we have so extensive a view.

'Yes,' said she, 'it is a very fine view indeed for a
flat country.'

'While, on the other hand, Mrs. B. gave us such a
dismal account of the precipices, mountains, and deserts
she encountered, that you would have thought she had
been on the wildest part of the Alps.'

The old Hampstead highroad, starting from the plain,
winds its way resolutely up the steep, and brings you past
red-brick houses and walled-in gardens to this noble out-
look ; to the heath, with its fresh, inspiriting breezes, its
lovely distances of far-off waters and gorsy hollows.    At
whatever season, at whatever hour you come, you are
pretty sure to find one or two votaries—poets like Mrs.
Barbauld, or commonplace people such as her friends—
watching before this great altar of nature ; whether by early
morning rays, or in the blazing sunset, or when the even-

ing veils and mists with stars come falling, while the lights
of London shine far away in the valley. Years after Mrs.
Barbauld wrote, one man, pre-eminent amongst poets, used
to stand upon this hill-top, and lo! as Turner gazed, a
whole generation gazed with him. For him Italy gleamed
from behind the crimson stems of the fir-trees; the spirit
of loveliest mythology floated upon the clouds, upon the
many changing tints of the plains; and, as the painter
watched the lights upon the distant hills, they sank into
his soul, and he painted them down for us, and poured
his dreams into our awakening hearts.

He was one of that race of giants, mighty men of
humble heart, who have looked from Hampstead and
Highgate Hills. Here Wordsworth trod; here sang
Keats's nightingale; here mused Coleridge; and here came
Carlyle, only yesterday, tramping wearily, in search of
some sign of his old companions. Here, too, stood kind
Walter Scott, under the elms of the Judges' Walk, and
perhaps Joanna Baillie was by his side, coming out from
her pretty old house beyond the trees. Besides all these,
were a whole company of lesser stars following and surrounding the brighter planets—muses, memoirs, critics,
poets, nymphs, authoresses—coming to drink tea and
to admire the pleasant suburban beauties of this modern
Parnassus. A record of many of their names is still

to be found, appropriately enough, in the catalogue
of the little Hampstead library which still exists, which
was founded at a time when the very hands that wrote the
books may have placed the old volumes upon the shelves.
Present readers can study them at their leisure, to the
clanking of the horses' feet in the courtyard outside, and
the splashing of buckets.  A few newspapers lie on the
table—stray sheets of to-day that have fluttered up the
hill, bringing news of this bustling now into a past
serenity.  The librarian sits stitching quietly in a window.
An old lady comes in to read the news ; but she has forgotten her spectacles, and soon goes away.  Here, instead
of asking for ' Vice Versâ,' or Ouida's last novel, you instinctively mention ' Plays of the Passions,' Miss Burney's
' Evelina,' or some such novels ; and Mrs. Barbauld's works
are also in their place.  When I asked for them, two
pretty old Quaker volumes were put into my hands, with
shabby grey bindings, with fine paper and broad margins,
such as Mr. Ruskin would approve.  Of all the inhabitants
of this bookshelf Mrs. Barbauld is one of the most appro-
priate.  It is but a few minutes' walk from the library in
Heath Street to the old corner house in Church Row where
she lived for a time, near a hundred years ago, and all
round about are the scenes of much of her life, of her
friendships and interests.  Here lived her friends and

neighbours; here to Church Row came her pupils and admirers, and, later still, to the pretty old house on Rosslyn Hill. As for Church Row, as most people know, it is an avenue of Dutch red-faced houses, leading demurely to the old church tower, that stands guarding its graves in the flowery churchyard. As we came up the quiet place, the sweet windy drone of the organ swelled across the blossoms of the spring, which were lighting up every shabby corner and hillside garden. Through this pleasant confusion of past and present, of spring-time scattering blossoms upon the graves, of old ivy walks and iron bars imprisoning past memories, with fragrant fumes of lilac and of elder, one could picture to oneself, as in a waking dream, two figures advancing from the corner house with the ivy walls—distinct, sedate—passing under the old doorway. I could almost see the lady, carefully dressed in many fine muslin folds and frills with hooped silk skirts, indeed, but slight and graceful in her quick advance, with blue eyes, with delicate sharp features, and a dazzling skin. As for the gentleman, I pictured him a dapper figure, with dark eyes, dressed in black, as befitted a minister even of dissenting views. The lady came forward, looking amused by my scrutiny, somewhat shy I thought—was she going to speak? And by the same token it seemed to me the gentleman was about to interrupt her. But Margaret, my

young companion, laughed and opened an umbrella, or a
cock crew, or some door banged, and the fleeting visions
of fancy disappeared.

Many well-authenticated ghost stories describe the
apparition of bygone persons, and lo! when the figure
vanishes, a letter is left behind! Some such experience
seemed to be mine when, on my return, I found a packet
of letters on the hall table—letters not addressed to me,
but to some unknown Miss Belsham, and signed and sealed
by Mrs. Barbauld's hand. They had been sent for me to
read by the kindness of some ladies now living at Hampstead, who afterwards showed me the portrait of the lady,
who began the world as Miss Betsy Belsham and who
ended her career as Mrs. Kenrick. It is an oval miniature,
belonging to the times of powder and of puff, representing
not a handsome, but an animated countenance, with
laughter and spirit in the expression; the mouth is large,
the eyes are dark, the nose is short. This was the *confi-*
*dante* of Mrs. Barbauld's early days, the faithful friend of
her latter sorrows. The letters, kept by 'Betsy' with
faithful conscientious care for many years, give the story
of a whole lifetime with unconscious fidelity. The gaiety
of youth, its impatience, its exuberance, and sometimes
bad taste; the wider, quieter feelings of later life; the
courage of sorrowful times; long friendship deepening the

tender and faithful memories of age, when there is so little left to say, so much to feel—all these things are there.

## II.

Mrs. Barbauld was a schoolmistress, and a schoolmaster's wife and daughter. Her father was Dr. John Aikin, D.D.; her mother was Miss Jane Jennings, of a good Northamptonshire family—scholastic also. Dr. Aikin brought his wife home to Knibworth, in Leicestershire, where he opened a school which became very successful in time. Mrs. Barbauld, their eldest child, was born here in 1743, and was christened Anna Lætitia, after some lady of high degree belonging to her mother's family. Two or three years later came a son. It was a quiet home, deep hidden in the secluded rural place; and the little household lived its own tranquil life far away from the storms and battles and great events that were stirring the world. Dr. Aikin kept school; Mrs. Aikin ruled her household with capacity, and not without some sternness, according to the custom of the time. It appears that late in life the good lady was distressed by the backwardness of her grandchildren at four or five years old. ' I once, indeed, knew a little girl,' so wrote Mrs. Aikin of her daughter, ' who was as eager to learn as her instructor could be to teach her, and who at two years old could read sentences and little stories, in her *wise* book, roundly and without spelling, and in half a year or more could read as well as most women; but I never knew such another, and I believe I never shall.' It was fortunate that no great harm came of this premature forcing, although it is difficult to say what its absence might not have done for Mrs. Barbauld. One can fancy the little assiduous girl, industrious, impulsive, interested in everything—in all life and all nature—drinking in, on every side, learning, eagerly wondering, listening to all around with bright and ready wit. There is a pretty little story told by Mrs. Ellis in her book about Mrs. Barbauld, how one day, when Dr. Aikin and a friend ' were conversing on the passions,' the Doctor observes that joy cannot have place in a state of perfect felicity, since it supposes an accession of happiness.

' I think you are mistaken, papa,' says a little voice from the opposite side of the table.

' Why so, my child ? ' says the Doctor.

' Because in the chapter I read to you this morning, in the Testament, it is said that " there is more joy in heaven over one sinner that repenteth than over ninety and nine just persons that need no repentance." '

Besides her English Testament and her early reading, the little girl was taught by her mother to do as little daughters did in those days, to obey a somewhat austere rule, to drop curtsies in the right place, to make beds, to preserve fruits. The father, after demur, but surely not without some paternal pride in her proficiency, taught the child Latin and French and Italian, and something of Greek, and gave her an acquaintance with English literature. One can imagine little Nancy with her fair head bending over her lessons, or, when playing time had come, perhaps a little lonely and listening to the distant voices of the schoolboys at their games. The mother, fearing she might acquire rough and boisterous manners, strictly forbade any communication with the schoolboys. Sometimes in after days, speaking of these early times and of the constraint of many bygone rules and regulations, Mrs. Barbauld used to attribute to this early formal training something of the hesitation and shyness which troubled her and never entirely wore off. She does not seem to have been in any great harmony with her mother. One could imagine a fanciful and high-spirited child, timid and dutiful, and yet strong-willed, secretly rebelling against the rigid order of her home, and feeling lonely for want of liberty and companionship. It was true she had birds and beasts and plants for her playfellows, but she was of a gregarious and sociable nature, and she was unconsciously longing for something more, and perhaps feeling a

want in her early life which no silent company can
supply.

She was about fifteen when a great event took place.
Her father was appointed classical tutor to the Warrington
Academy, and thither the little family removed. We
read that the Warrington Academy was a Dissenting
college started by very eminent and periwigged personages, whose silhouettes Mrs. Barbauld herself afterwards
cut out in sticking-plaster, and whose names are to this
day remembered and held in just esteem. They were
people of simple living and high thinking, they belonged
to a class holding then a higher place than now in the
world's esteem, that of Dissenting ministers. The Dissenting ministers were fairly well paid and faithfully
followed by their congregations. The college was started
under the auspices of distinguished members of the
community, Lord Willoughby of Parham, the last
Presbyterian lord, being patron. Among the masters
were to be found the well-known names of Dr. Doddridge;
of Gilbert Wakefield, the reformer and uncompromising
martyr; of Dr. Taylor, of Norwich, the Hebrew scholar;
of Dr. Priestley, the chemical analyst and patriot, and
enterprising theologian, who left England and settled in
America for conscience and liberty's sake.

Many other people, neither students nor professors,

used to come to Warrington, and chief among them in later years good John Howard with MSS. for his friend Dr. Aikin to correct for the press. Now for the first time Mrs. Barbauld (Miss Aikin she was then) saw something of real life, of men and manners. It was not likely that she looked back with any lingering regret to Knibworth, or would have willingly returned thither. A story in one of her memoirs gives an amusing picture of the manners of a young country lady of that day. Mr. Haines, a rich farmer from Knibworth, who had been greatly struck by Miss Aikin, followed her to Warrington, and 'obtained a private audience of her father and begged his consent to be allowed to make her his wife.' The father answered 'that his daughter was there walking in the garden, and he might go and ask her himself.' ' With what grace the farmer pleaded his cause I know not,' says her biographer and niece. ' Out of all patience at his unwelcome importunities, my aunt ran nimbly up a tree which grew by the garden wall, and let herself down into the lane beyond.'

The next few years must have been perhaps the happiest of Mrs. Barbauld's life. Once when it was nearly over she said to her niece, Mrs. Le Breton, from whose interesting account I have been quoting, that she had never been placed in a situation which really suited her. As one reads her sketches and poems, one is struck

by some sense of this detracting influence of which she
complains: there is a certain incompleteness and slight-
ness which speaks of intermittent work, of interrupted
trains of thought.  At the same time there is a natural
buoyant quality in much of her writing which seems like
a pleasant landscape view seen through the bars of a
window.  There may be wider prospects, but her eyes are
bright, and this peep of nature is undoubtedly delightful.

### III.

The letters to Miss Belsham begin somewhere about
1768.  The young lady has been paying a visit to Miss
Aikin at Warrington, and is interested in everyone and
everything belonging to the place.  Miss Aikin is no less
eager to describe than Miss Belsham to listen, and
accordingly a whole stream of characters and details of
gossip and descriptions in faded ink come flowing across
their pages, together with many expressions of affection
and interest.  'My dear Betsy, I love you for discarding
the word Miss from your vocabulary,' so the packet begins,
and it continues in the same strain of pleasant girlish
chatter, alternating with the history of many bygone
festivities, and stories of friends, neighbours, of beaux and
partners; of the latter genus, and of Miss Aikin's efforts

to make herself agreeable, here is a sample :—' I talked to him, smiled upon him, gave him my fan to play with,' says the lively young lady. 'Nothing would do; he was grave as a philosopher. I tried to raise a conversation : " 'Twas fine weather for dancing." He agreed to my observation. " We had a tolerable set this time." Neither did he contradict that. Then we were both silent—stupid mortal thought I! but unreasonable as he appeared to the advances that I made him, there was one object in the room, a sparkling object which seemed to attract all his attention, on which he seemed to gaze with transport, and which indeed he hardly took his eyes off the whole time . . . . The object that I mean was his shoebuckle.'

One could imagine Miss Elizabeth Bennett writing in some such strain to her friend Miss Charlotte Lucas after one of the evenings at Bingley's hospitable mansion. And yet Miss Aikin is more impulsive, more romantic than Elizabeth. 'Wherever you are, fly letter on the wings of the wind,' she cries, 'and tell my dear Betsy what ?—only that I love her dearly.'

Miss Nancy Aikin (she seems to have been Nancy in these letters, and to have assumed the more dignified Lætitia upon her marriage) pours out her lively heart, laughs, jokes, interests herself in the sentimental affairs

of the whole neighbourhood as well as in her own.
Perhaps few young ladies now-a-days would write to their
*confidantes* with the announcement that for some time
past a young sprig had been teasing them to have him.
This, however, is among Miss Nancy's confidences. She
also writes poems and *jeux d'esprit,* and receives poetry
in return from Betsy, who calls herself Camilla, and
pays her friend many compliments, for Miss Aikin in her
reply quotes the well-known lines :—

> Who for another's brow entwines the bays,
> And where she well might rival stoops to Praise.

Miss Aikin by this time has attained to all the dignity of
a full-blown authoress, and is publishing a successful book
of poems in conjunction with her brother, which little
book created much attention at the time. One day the
Muse thus apostrophises Betsy : 'Shall we ever see her
amongst us again?' says my sister (Mrs. Aikin). My
brother (saucy fellow) says, 'I want to see this girl, I think
(stroking his chin as he walks backwards and forwards in
the room with great gravity). I think we should admire
one another.

'When you come among us,' continues the warm-
hearted friend, ' we shall set the bells a-ringing, bid adieu
to care and gravity, and sing " O be joyful." ' And finally,

after some apologies for her remiss correspondence, ' I left my brother writing to you instead of Patty, poor soul. Well, it is a clever thing too, to have a husband to write one's letters for one. If I had one I would be a much better correspondent to you. I would order him to write every week.'

And, indeed, Mrs. Barbauld was as good as her word, and did not forget the resolutions made by Miss Aikin in 1773. In 1774 comes some eventful news : ' I should have written to you sooner had it not been for the uncertainty and suspense in which for a long time I have been involved ; and since my lot has been fixed for many busy engagements which have left me few moments of leisure. They hurry me out of my life. It is hardly a month that I have certainly known I should fix on Norfolk, and now next Thursday they say I am to be finally, irrevocably married. Pity me, dear Betsy ; for on the day I fancy when you will read this letter, will the event take place which is to make so great an era in my life. I feel depressed, and my courage almost fails me. Yet upon the whole I have the greatest reason to think I shall be happy. shall possess the entire affection of a worthy man, whom my father and mother now entirely and heartily approve. The people where we are going, though strangers, have behaved with the greatest zeal and affection ; and I think

we have a fair prospect of being useful and living comfortably in that state of middling life to which I have been
accustomed, and which I love.'

And then comes a word which must interest all who
have ever cared and felt grateful admiration for the works
of one devoted human being and true Christian hero.
Speaking of her father's friend, John Howard, she says
with an almost audible sigh: ' It was too late, as you say,
or I believe I should have been in love with Mr. Howard.
Seriously, I looked upon him with that sort of reverence and
love which one should have for a guardian angel. God bless
him and preserve his health for the health's sake of thou-
sands. And now farewell,' she writes in conclusion: ' I
shall write to you no more under this name ; but under any
name, in every situation, at any distance of time or place,
I shall love you equally and be always affectionately yours,
tho' *not* always, A. AIKIN.'

Poor lady ! The future held, indeed, many a sad and
unsuspected hour for her, many a cruel pang, many a dark
and heavy season, that must have seemed intolerably
weary to one of her sprightly and yet somewhat indolent
nature, more easily accepting evil than devising escape
from it. But it also held many blessings of constancy,
friendship, kindly deeds, and useful doings. She had not

devotion to give such as that of the good Howard whom
she revered, but the equable help and sympathy for
others of an open-minded and kindly woman was hers.
Her marriage would seem to have been brought about
by a romantic fancy rather than by a tender affection.
Mr. Barbauld's mind had been once unhinged ; his pro-
testations were passionate and somewhat dramatic. We
are told that when she was warned by a friend, she only
said, ' But surely, if I throw him over, he will become
crazy again ; ' and from a high-minded sense of pity, she
was faithful, and married him against the wish of her
brother and parents, and not without some misgivings herself. He was a man perfectly sincere and honourable ;
but, from his nervous want of equilibrium, subject all his
life to frantic outbursts of ill-temper. Nobody ever knew
what his wife had to endure in secret ; her calm and
restrained manner must have effectually hidden the constant anxiety of her life ; nor had she children to warm
her heart, and brighten up her monotonous existence.
Little Charles, of the Reading-book, who is bid to come
hither, who counted so nicely, who stroked the pussy cat,
and who deserved to listen to the delightful stories he was
told, was not her own son but her brother's child. When
he was born, she wrote to entreat that he might be given
over to her for her own, imploring her brother to spare him

to her, in a pretty and pathetic letter.   This was a mother
yearning for a child, not a schoolmistress asking for a
pupil, though perhaps in after times the two were somewhat
combined in her.   There is a pretty little description of
Charles making great progress in ' climbing trees and
talking nonsense : ' ' I have the honour to tell you that our
Charles is the sweetest boy in the world.   He is perfectly
naturalised in his new situation ; and if I should make any
blunders in my letter, I must beg you to impute it to his
standing by me and chattering all the time.'   And how
pleasant a record exists of Charles's chatter in that most
charming little book written for him and for the babies of
babies to come !   There is a sweet instructive grace in it
and appreciation of childhood which cannot fail to strike
those who have to do with children and with Mrs. Barbauld's
books for them : children themselves, those best critics of
all, delight in it.

' Where's Charles ? ' says a little scholar every morning
to the writer of these few notes.


## IV.

Soon after the marriage, there had been some thought
of a college for young ladies, of which Mrs. Barbauld was
to be the principal ; but she shrank from the idea, and in a

letter to Mrs. Montagu she objects to the scheme of higher education for women away from their natural homes. ' I should have little hope of cultivating a love of knowledge in a young lady of fifteen who came to me ignorant and uncultivated. It is too late then to begin to learn. The empire of the passions is coming on. Those attachments begin to be formed which influence the happiness of future life. The care of a mother alone can give suitable attention to this important period.' It is true that the rigidness of her own home had not prevented her from making a hasty and unsuitable marriage. But it is not this which is weighing on her mind. ' Perhaps you may think,' she says, 'that having myself stepped out of the bounds of female reserve in becoming an author, it is with an ill grace that I offer these statements.'

Her arguments seem to have been thought conclusive in those days, and the young ladies' college was finally transmuted into a school for little boys at Palgrave, in Norfolk, and thither the worthy couple transported themselves.

One of the letters to Miss Belsham is thus dated :—
' *The 14th of July, in the village of Palgrave (the pleasantest village in all England), at ten o'clock, all alone in my great parlour, Mr. Barbauld being studying a sermon, do I begin a letter to my dear Betsy.*'

When she first married, and travelled into Norfolk to

keep school at Palgrave, nothing could have seemed more
tranquil, more contented, more matter-of-fact than her life
as it appears from her letters.    Dreams, and fancies, and
gay illusions and excitements have made way for the
somewhat disappointing realisation of Mr. Barbauld with
his neatly turned and friendly postscripts—a husband,
polite, devoted, it is true, but somewhat disappointing all
the same.    The next few years seem like years in a hive
—storing honey for the future, and  putting away—industrious, punctual, monotonous.    There are children's
lessons to be heard, and school-treats to be devised.    She
sets them to act plays and cuts out paper collars for
Henry IV. ; she always takes a class of babies entirely her
own.    (One of these babies, who always loved her, became
Lord Chancellor Denman ; most of the others took less
brilliant, but equally respectable places, in after life.)
She has also household matters and correspondence not to
be neglected.    In the holidays, they make excursions to
Norwich, to London, and revisit their old haunts at
Warrington.    In one of her early letters, soon after her
marriage, she describes her return to Warrington.

     ' Dr. Enfield's face,' she declares, ' is grown half a foot
longer since I saw him, with studying mathematics, and
for want of a game of romps; for there are positively
none now at Warrington but grave matrons.    I who

have but half assumed the character, was ashamed of the levity of my behaviour.'

It says well indeed for the natural brightness of the lady's disposition that with sixteen boarders and a satisfactory usher to look after, she should be prepared for a game of romps with Dr. Enfield.

On another occasion, in 1777, she takes little Charles away with her. ' He has indeed been an excellent traveller,' she says; 'and though, like his great ancestor, some natural tears he shed, like him, too, he wiped them soon. He had a long sound sleep last night, and has been very busy to-day hunting the puss and the chickens. And now, my dear brother and sister, let me again thank you for this precious gift, the value of which we are both more and more sensible of as we become better acquainted with his sweet disposition and winning manners.'

She winds up this letter with a postscript :—

' Everybody here asks, " Pray, is Dr. Dodd really to be executed ? " as if we knew the more for having been at Warrington.'

Dr. Aikin, Mrs. Barbauld's brother, the father of little Charles and of Lucy Aikin, whose name is well known in literature, was himself a man of great' parts, industry, and ability, working hard to support his family. He alternated between medicine and literature all his life.

When his health failed he gave up medicine, and settled at Stoke Newington, and busied himself with periodic literature; meanwhile, whatever his own pursuits may have been, he never ceased to take an interest in his sister's work and to encourage her in every way.

It is noteworthy that few of Mrs. Barbauld's earlier productions equalled what she wrote at the very end of her life. She seems to have been one of those who ripen with age, growing wider in spirit with increasing years. Perhaps, too, she may have been influenced by the change of manners, the reaction against formalism, which was growing up as her own days were ending. Prim she may have been in manner, but she was not a formalist by nature; and even at eighty was ready to learn to submit to accept the new gospel that Wordsworth and his disciples had given to the world, and to shake off the stiffness of early training.

It is idle to speculate on what might have been if things had happened otherwise; if the daily stress of anxiety and perplexity which haunted her home had been removed—difficulties and anxieties which may well have absorbed all the spare energy and interest that under happier circumstances might have added to the treasury of English literature. But if it were only for one ode written when the distracting cares of over seventy years

were ending, when nothing remained to her but the
essence of a long past, and the inspirations of a still
glowing, still hopeful, and most tender spirit, if it were
only for the ode called ' Life,' which has brought a sense
of ease and comfort to so many, Mrs. Barbauld has indeed
deserved well of her country-people and should be held in
remembrance by them.

Her literary works are, after all, not very voluminous.
She is best known by her hymns for children and her
early lessons, than which nothing more childlike has ever
been devised ; and we can agree with her brother, Dr.
Aikin, when he says that it requires true genius to enter
so completely into a child's mind.

After their first volume of verse, the brother and sister
had published a second in prose, called ' Miscellaneous
Pieces,' about which there is an amusing little anecdote in
Rogers's ' Memoirs.' Fox met Dr. Aikin at dinner.

' " I am greatly pleased with your ' Miscellaneous
Pieces,' " said Fox. Aikin bowed. " I particularly admire,"
continued Fox, " your essay ' Against Inconsistency in our
Expectations.' "

' " That," replied Aikin, " is my sister's."

' " I like much," returned Fox, " your essay ' On Mo-
nastic Institutions.' "

' " That," answered Aikin, " is also my sister's."

' Fox thought it best to say no more about the book.'

These essays were followed by various of the visions and Eastern pieces then so much in vogue; also by political verses and pamphlets, which seemed to have made a great sensation at the time. But Mrs. Barbauld's turn was on the whole more for domestic than for literary life, although literary people always seem to have had a great interest for her.

During one Christmas which they spent in London, the worthy couple go to see Mrs. Siddons; and Mrs. Chapone introduces Mrs. Barbauld to Miss Burney. ' A very unaffected, modest, sweet, and pleasing young lady,' says Mrs. Barbauld, who is always kind in her descriptions. Mrs. Barbauld's one complaint in London is of the fatigue from hairdressers, and the bewildering hurry of the great city, where she had, notwithstanding her quiet country life, many ties, and friendships, and acquaintances. Her poem on ' Corsica' had brought her into some relations with Boswell; she also knew Goldsmith and Dr. Johnson. Here is her description of the ' Great Bear : '—

' I do not mean that one which shines in the sky over your head; but the Bear that shines in London—a great rough, surly animal. His Christian name is Dr. Johnson. 'Tis a singular creature; but if you stroke him he will

not bite, and though he growls sometimes he is not ill-
humoured.'

Johnson describes Mrs. Barbauld as suckling fools and
chronicling small beer. There was not much sympathy
between the two. Characters such as Johnson's harmonise
best with the enthusiastic and easily influenced. Mrs.
Barbauld did not belong to this class; she trusted to her
own judgment, rarely tried to influence others, and took a
matter-of-fact rather than a passionate view of life. She
is as severe to him in her criticism as he was in his judgment of her : they neither of them did the other justice.
' A Christian and a man-about-town, a philosopher, and a
bigot acknowledging life to be miserable, and making it
more miserable through fear of death.' So she writes of
him, and all this was true; but how much more was also
true of the great and hypochondriacal old man! Some
years afterwards, when she had been reading Boswell's
long-expected ' Life of Johnson,' she wrote of the book :—
' It is like going to Ranelagh; you meet all your acquaintances; but it is a base and mean thing to bring thus
every idle word into judgment.' In our own day we too
have our Boswell and our Johnson to arouse discussion and
indignation.

' Have you seen Boswell's " Life of Johnson ?" He calls
it a Flemish portrait, and so it is—two quartos of a man's

conversation and petty habits. Then the treachery and meanness of watching a man for years in order to set down every unguarded and idle word he uttered, is inconceivable. Yet with all this one cannot help reading a good deal of it.' This is addressed to the faithful Betsy, who was also keeping school by that time, and assuming brevet rank in consequence.

Mrs. Barbauld might well complain of the fatigue from hairdressers in London. In one of her letters to her friend she thus describes a lady's dress of the period :—

' Do you know how to dress yourself in Dublin? If you do not, I will tell you. Your waist must be the circumference of two oranges, no more. You must erect a structure on your head gradually ascending to a foot high, exclusive of feathers, and stretching to a penthouse of most horrible projection behind, the breadth from wing to wing considerably broader than your shoulder, and as many different things in your cap as in Noah's ark. Verily, I never did see such monsters as the heads now in vogue. I am a monster, too, but a moderate one.'

She must have been glad to get back to her home, to her daily work, to Charles, climbing his trees and talking his nonsense.

In the winter of 1784 her mother died at Palgrave. It was Christmas week ; the old lady had come travelling

four days through the snow in a postchaise with her
maid and her little grandchildren, while her son rode on
horseback. But the cold and the fatigue of the journey,
and the discomfort of the inns, proved too much for Mrs.
Aikin, who reached her daughter's house only to die. Just
that time three years before Mrs. Barbauld had lost her
father, whom she dearly loved. There is a striking letter
from the widowed mother to her daughter recording the
event. It is almost Spartan in its calmness, but nevertheless deeply touching. Now she, too, was at rest, and after
Mrs. Aikin's death a cloud of sadness and depression seems
to have fallen upon the household. Mr. Barbauld was
ailing; he was suffering from a nervous irritability
which occasionally quite unfitted him for his work as a
schoolmaster. Already his wife must have had many
things to bear, and very much to try her courage and
cheerfulness; and now her health was also failing. It was
in 1775 that they gave up the academy, which, on the
whole, had greatly flourished. It had been established
eleven years; they were both of them in need of rest and
change. Nevertheless, it was not without reluctance that
they brought themselves to leave their home at Palgrave.
A successor was found only too quickly for Mrs. Barbauld's
wishes; they handed over their pupils to his care, and
went abroad for a year's sunshine and distraction.

## V.

What a contrast to prim, starched scholastic life at Palgrave must have been the smiling world, and the land flowing with oil and wine, in which they found themselves basking! The vintage was so abundant that year that the country people could not find vessels to contain it. 'The roads covered with teams of casks, empty or full according as they were going out or returning, and drawn by oxen whose strong necks seemed to be bowed unwillingly under the yoke. Men, women, and children were abroad; some cutting with a short sickle the bunches of grapes, some breaking them with a wooden instrument, some carrying them on their backs from the gatherers to those who pressed the juice; and, as in our harvest, the gleaners followed.'

From the vintage they travel to the Alps, 'a sight so majestic, so totally different from anything I had seen before, that I am ready to sing *nunc dimittis*,' she writes. They travel back by the south of France and reach Paris in June, where the case of the Diamond Necklace is being tried. Then they return to England, waiting a day at Boulogne for a vessel, but crossing from thence in less than four hours. How pretty is her description of England as it strikes them after their absence! 'And not without

pleasing emotion did we view again the green swelling
hills covered with large sheep, and the winding road
bordered with the hawthorn hedge, and the English vine
twirled round the tall poles, and the broad Medway covered
with vessels, and at last the gentle yet majestic Thames.'

There were Dissenters at Hampstead in those days, as
there are still, and it was a call from a little Unitarian
congregation on the hillside who invited Mrs. Barbauld to
become their minister, which decided the worthy couple to
retire to this pleasant suburb.   The place seemed promising
enough ; they were within reach of Mrs. Barbauld's brother,
Dr. Aikin, now settled in London, and to whom she was
tenderly attached.   There were congenial people settled
all about.   On the high hill-top were pleasant old houses
to live in.   There was occupation for him and literary
interest for her.

They are a sociable and friendly pair, hospitable, glad
to welcome their friends, and the acquaintance, and critics,
and the former pupils who come toiling up the hill to visit
them.   Rogers comes to dinner 'at half after three.'   They
have another poet for a neighbour, Miss Joanna Baillie ;
they are made welcome by all, and in their turn make
others welcome ; they do acts of social charity and kindness
wherever they see the occasion.   They have a young
Spanish gentleman to board who conceals a taste for

'seguars.' They also go up to town from time to time.
On one occasion Mr. Barbauld repairs to London to choose
a wedding present for Miss Belsham, who is about to be
married to Mr. Kenrick, a widower with daughters.   He
chose two slim Wedgwood pots of some late classic
model, which still stand, after many dangers, safely on
either side of Mrs. Kenrick's portrait in Miss Reid's drawing-room at Hampstead.   Wedgwood must have been a
personal friend : he has modelled a lovely head of Mrs.
Barbauld, simple and nymph-like.

Hampstead was no further from London in those days
than it is now, and they seem to have kept up a constant
communication with their friends and relations in the
great city.   They go to the play occasionally.   'I have
not indeed seen Mrs. Siddons often, but I think I never saw
her to more advantage,' she writes.   'It is not, however,
seeing a play, it is only seeing one character, for they have
nobody to act with her.'

Another expedition is to Westminster Hall, where
Warren Hastings was then being tried for his life.

'The trial has attracted the notice of most people who
are within reach of it.   I have been, and was very much
struck with all the apparatus and pomp of justice, with
the splendour of the assembly which contained everything
distinguished in the nation, with the grand idea that the

equity of the English was to pursue crimes committed at the other side of the globe, and oppressions exercised towards the poor Indians who had come to plead their cause; but all these fine ideas vanish and fade away as one observes the progress of the cause, and sees it fall into the summer amusements, and take the place of a rehearsal of music or an evening at Vauxhall.'

Mrs. Barbauld was a Liberal in feeling and conviction; she was never afraid to speak her mind, and when the French Revolution first began, she, in common with many others, hoped that it was but the dawning of happier times. She was always keen about public events; she wrote an address on the opposition to the repeal of the Test Act in 1791, and she published her poem to Wilberforce on the rejection of his great bill for abolishing slavery:—

Friends of the friendless, hail, ye generous band!

she cries, in warm enthusiasm for the devoted cause.

Horace Walpole nicknamed her Deborah, called her the Virago Barbauld, and speaks of her with utter rudeness and intolerant spite. But whether or not Horace Walpole approved, it is certain that Mrs. Barbauld possessed to a full and generous degree a quality which is now less common than it was in her day.

Not very many years ago I was struck on one occasion when a noble old lady, now gone to her rest, exclaimed in my hearing that people of this generation had all sorts of merits and charitable intentions, but that there was one thing she missed which had certainly existed in her youth, and which no longer seemed to be of the same account: that public spirit which used to animate the young as well as the old.

It is possible that philanthropy, and the love of the beautiful, and the gratuitous diffusion of wall-papers may be the modern rendering of the good old-fashioned sentiment. Mrs. Barbauld lived in very stirring days, when private people shared in the excitements and catastrophes of public affairs. To her the fortunes of England, its loyalty, its success, were a part of her daily bread. By her early associations she belonged to a party representing opposition, and for that very reason she was the more keenly struck by the differences of the conduct of affairs and the opinions of those she trusted. Her friend Dr. Priestley had emigrated to America for his convictions' sake; Howard was giving his noble life for his work; Wakefield had gone to prison. Now the very questions are forgotten for which they struggled and suffered, or the answers have come while the questions are forgotten, in this their future which is our present, and to which

some unborn historian may point back with a moral
finger.

Dr. Aikin, whose estimate of his sister was very different
from Horace Walpole's, occasionally reproached her for not
writing more constantly. He wrote a copy of verses on
this theme :—

> Thus speaks the Muse, and bends her brows severe :
> Did I, Lætitia, lend my choicest lays,
> And crown thy youthful head with freshest bays,
> That all the expectance of thy full-grown year,
> Should lie inert and fruitless ? O revere
> Those sacred gifts whose meed is deathless praise,
> Whose potent charm the enraptured soul can raise
> Far from the vapours of this earthly sphere,
> Seize, seize the lyre, resume the lofty strain.

She seems to have willingly left the lyre for Dr. Aikin's
use. A few hymns, some graceful odes, and stanzas, and
*jeux d'esprit*, a certain number of well-written and original
essays, and several political pamphlets, represent the best
of her work. Her more ambitious poems are those by
which she is the least remembered. It was at Hampstead
that Mrs. Barbauld wrote her contributions to her brother's
volume of 'Evenings at Home,' among which the trans-
migrations of Indur may be quoted as a model of style
and delightful matter. One of the best of her *jeux d'esprit*
is the 'Groans of the Tankard,' which was written in early

days, with much spirit and real humour. It begins with a classic incantation, and then goes on :—

> 'Twas at the solemn silent noontide hour
> When hunger rages with despotic power,
> When the lean student quits his Hebrew roots
> For the gross nourishment of English fruits,
> And throws unfinished airy systems by
> For solid pudding and substantial pie.

The tankard now,

> Replenished to the brink,
> With the cool beverage blue-eyed maidens drink,

but, accustomed to very different libations, is endowed with voice and utters its bitter reproaches :—

> Unblest the day, and luckless was the hour
> Which doomed me to a Presbyterian's power,
> Fated to serve a Puritanic race,
> Whose slender meal is shorter than their grace.

## VI.

Thumbkin, of fairy celebrity, used to mark his way by flinging crumbs of bread and scattering stones as he went along; and in like manner authors trace the course of their life's peregrinations by the pamphlets and articles they cast down as they go. Sometimes they throw stones, sometimes they throw bread. In '92 and '93 Mrs. Barbauld must have been occupied with party polemics and with the political miseries of the time. A pamphlet on Gilbert Wakefield's views, and another on 'Sins of the Government and Sins of the People,' show in what direction her thoughts were bent. Then came a period of comparative calm again and of literary work and interest. She seems to have turned to Akenside and Collins, and each had an essay to himself. These were followed by certain selections from the *Spectator*, *Tatler*, &c., preceded by one of those admirable essays for which she is really remarkable. She also published a memoir of Richardson prefixed to his correspondence. Sir James Mackintosh, writing at a later and sadder time of her life, says of her observations on the moral of Clarissa that they are as fine a piece of mitigated and rational stoicism as our language can boast of.

In 1802 another congregation seems to have made signs from Stoke Newington, and Mrs. Barbauld persuaded her husband to leave his flock at Hampstead and to buy a house near her brother's at Stoke Newington. This was her last migration, and here she remained until her death in 1825. One of her letters to Mrs. Kenrick gives a description of what might have been a happy home :—' We have a pretty little back parlour that looks into our little spot of a garden,' she says, ' and catches every gleam of sunshine. We have pulled down the ivy, except what covers the coach-house

We have planted a vine and a passion-flower, with abundance of jessamine against the window, and we have scattered roses and honeysuckle all over the garden.  You may smile at me for parading so over my house and domains.' In May she writes a pleasant letter, in good spirits, comparing her correspondence with her friend to the flower of an aloe, which sleeps for a hundred years, and on a sudden pushes out when least expected.  ' But take notice, the life is in the aloe all the while, and sorry should I be if the life were not in our friendship all the while, though it so rarely diffuses itself over a sheet of paper.'

She seems to have been no less sociable and friendly at Stoke Newington than at Hampstead.  People used to come up to see her from London.  Her letters, quiet and intimate as they are, give glimpses of most of the literary people of the day, not in memoirs then, but alive and drinking tea at one another's houses, or walking all the way to Stoke Newington to pay their respects to the old lady.

Charles Lamb used to talk of his two *bald* authoresses, Mrs. Barbauld being one and Mrs. Inchbald being the other. Crabb Robinson and Rogers were two faithful links with the outer world.  'Crabb Robinson corresponds with Madame de Staël, is quite intimate,' she writes, ' has received I don't know how many letters,' she adds, not without some slight amusement.  Miss Lucy Aikin tells a pretty story

of Scott meeting Mrs. Barbauld at dinner, and telling her
that it was to her that he owed his poetic gift. Some
translations of Bürger by Mr. Taylor, of Norwich, which
she had read out at Edinburgh, had struck him so much
that they had determined him to try his own powers in
that line.

She often had inmates under her roof. One of them
was a beautiful and charming young girl, the daughter of
Mrs. Fletcher, of Edinburgh, whose early death is recorded
in her mother's life. Besides company at home, Mrs. Barbauld went to visit her friends from time to time—the
Estlins at Bristol, the Edgeworths, whose acquaintance Mr.
and Mrs. Barbauld made about this time, and who seem to
have been invaluable friends, bringing as they did a bright
new element of interest and cheerful friendship into her
sad and dimning life. A man must have extraordinarily
good spirits to embark upon four matrimonial ventures as
Mr. Edgeworth did; and as for Miss Edgeworth, appre-
ciative, effusive, and warm-hearted, she seems to have
more than returned Mrs. Barbauld's sympathy.

Miss Lucy Aikin, Dr. Aikin's daughter, was now also
making her own mark in the literary world, and had
inherited the bright intelligence and interest for which
her family was so remarkable. Much of Miss Aikin's
work is more sustained than her aunt's desultory pro-

ductions, but it lacks that touch of nature which has preserved Mrs. Barbauld's memory where more important people are forgotten.

Our authoress seems to have had a natural affection for sister authoresses. Hannah More and Mrs. Montague were both her friends, so were Madame d'Arblay and Mrs. Chapone in a different degree; she must have known Mrs. Opie; she loved Joanna Baillie. The latter is described by her as the young lady at Hampstead who came to Mr. Barbauld's meeting with as demure a face as if she had never written a line. And Miss Aikin, in her memoirs, describes in Johnsonian language how the two Miss Baillies came to call one morning upon Mrs. Barbauld:—' My aunt immediately introduced the topic of the anonymous tragedies, and gave utterance to her admiration with the generous delight in the manifestation of kindred genius which distinguished her.' But it seems that Miss Baillie sat, nothing moved, and did not betray herself. Mrs. Barbauld herself gives a pretty description of the sisters in their home, in that old house on Windmill Hill, which stands untouched, with its green windows looking out upon so much of sky and heath and sun, with the wainscoted parlours where Walter Scott used to come, and the low wooden staircase leading to the old rooms above. It is in one of her letters to Mrs. Kenrick that Mrs. Barbauld gives

a pleasant glimpse of the poetess Walter Scott admired.
' I have not been abroad since I was at Norwich, except a
day or two at Hampstead with the Miss Baillies.　One
should be, as I was, beneath their roof to know all their
merit.　Their house is one of the best ordered I know.
They have all manner of attentions for their friends, and
not only Miss B., but Joanna, is as clever in furnishing a
room or in arranging a party as in writing plays, of which,
by the way, she has a volume ready for the press, but she
will not give it to the public till next winter.　The subject
is to be the passion of fear.　I do not know what sort of
a hero that passion can afford ! '　Fear was, indeed, a passion
alien to her nature, and she did not know the meaning of
the word.

Mrs. Barbauld's description of Hannah More and her
sisters living on their special hill-top was written after
Mr. Barbauld's death, and thirty years after Miss More's
verses which are quoted by Mrs. Ellis in her excellent
memoir of Mrs. Barbauld :—

> Nor, Barbauld, shall my glowing heart refuse
> A tribute to thy virtues or thy muse ;
> This humble merit shall at least be mine,
> The poet's chaplet for thy brows to twine ;
> My verse thy talents to the world shall teach,
> And praise the graces it despairs to reach.

Then, after philosophically questioning the power of genius
to confer true happiness, she concludes :—

> Can all the boasted powers of wit and song
> Of life one pang remove, one hour prolong?
> Fallacious hope which daily truths deride—
> For you, alas! have wept and Garrick died.

Meanwhile, whatever genius might not be able to
achieve, the five Miss Mores had been living on peacefully
together in the very comfortable cottage which had been
raised and thatched by the poetess's earnings.

'Barley Wood is equally the seat of taste and hospitality,' says Mrs. Barbauld to a friend.

'Nothing could be more friendly than their reception,'
she writes to her brother, 'and nothing more charming
than their situation. An extensive view over the Mendip
Hills is in front of their house, with a pretty view of
Wrington. Their home—cottage, because it is thatched
—stands on the declivity of a rising ground, which they
have planted and made quite a little paradise. The five
sisters, all good old maids, have lived together these fifty
years. Hannah More is a good deal broken, but possesses
fully her powers of conversation, and her vivacity. We
exchanged riddles like the wise men of old; I was given
to understand she was writing something.'

There is another allusion to Mrs. Hannah More in a

sensible letter from Mrs. Barbauld, written to Miss Edgeworth about this time, declining to join in an alarming enterprise suggested by the vivacious Mr. Edgeworth, ' a *Feminiad,* a literary paper to be entirely contributed to by ladies, and where all articles are to be accepted.' ' There is no bond of union,' Mrs. Barbauld says, ' among literary women any more than among literary men ; different sentiments and connections separate them much more than the joint interest of their sex would unite them. Mrs. Hannah More would not write along with you or me, and we should possibly hesitate at joining Miss Hays or—if she were living—Mrs. Godwin.' Then she suggests the names of Miss Baillie, Mrs. Opie, her own niece Miss Lucy Aikin, and Mr. S. Rogers, who would not, she thinks, be averse to joining the scheme.

## VII.

How strangely unnatural it seems when Fate's heavy hand falls upon quiet and common-place lives, changing the tranquil routine of every day into the solemnities and excitements of terror and tragedy! It was after their removal to Stoke Newington that the saddest of all blows fell upon this true-hearted woman. Her husband's hypochondria deepened and changed, and the attacks became

so serious that her brother and his family urged her
anxiously to leave him to other care than her own. It
was no longer safe for poor Mr. Barbauld to remain alone
with his wife, and her life, says Mrs. Le Breton, was more
than once in peril. But, at first, she would not hear of
leaving him; although on more than one occasion she had
to fly for protection to her brother close by.

There is something very touching in the patient
fidelity with which Mrs. Barbauld tried to soothe the later
sad disastrous years of her husband's life. She must have
been a woman of singular nerve and courage to endure as
she did the excitement and cruel aberrations of her once
gentle and devoted companion. She only gave in after
long resistance.

'An alienation from me has taken possession of his
mind,' she says, in a letter to Mrs. Kenrick; 'my presence
seems to irritate him, and I must resign myself to a separation from him who has been for thirty years the partner
of my heart, my faithful friend, my inseparable companion.' With her habitual reticence, she dwells no
more on that painful topic, but goes on to make plans for
them both, asks her old friend to come and cheer her in
her loneliness; and the faithful Betsy, now a widow with
grown-up step-children, ill herself, troubled by deafness
and other infirmities, responds with a warm heart, and

promises to come, bringing the comfort with her of old companionship and familiar sympathy. There is something very affecting in the loyalty of the two aged women stretching out their hands to each other across a whole lifetime. After her visit Mrs. Barbauld writes again :—

'He is now at Norwich, and I hear very favourable accounts of his health and spirits ; he seems to enjoy himself very much amongst his old friends there, and converses among them with his usual animation. There are no symptoms of violence or of depression ; so far is favourable ; but this cruel alienation from me, in which my brother is included, still remains deep-rooted, and whether he will ever change in this point Heaven only knows. The medical men fear he will not : if so, my dear friend, what remains for me but to resign myself to the will of Heaven, and to think with pleasure that every day brings me nearer a period which naturally cannot be very far off, and at which this as well as every temporal affliction must terminate ?

' "Anything but this ! " is the cry of weak mortals when afflicted ; and sometimes I own I am inclined to make it mine ; but I will check myself.'

But while she was hoping still, a fresh outbreak of the malady occurred. He, poor soul, weary of his existence, put an end to his sufferings : he was found lifeless in the

New River.　Lucy Aikin quotes a Dirge found among her
aunt's papers after her death :—

> Pure Spirit, O where art thou now ?
> 　O whisper to my soul,
> O let some soothening thought of thee
> 　This bitter grief control.
>
> 'Tis not for thee the tears I shed,
> 　Thy sufferings now are o'er.
> The sea is calm, the tempest past,
> 　On that eternal shore.
>
> No more the storms that wrecked thy peace
> 　Shall tear that gentle breast,
> Nor summer's rage, nor winter's cold
> 　That poor, poor frame molest.
>
> 　.　　　　.　　　　.　　　　.
>
> Farewell ! With honour, peace, and love,
> 　Be that dear memory blest,
> Thou hast no tears for me to shed,
> 　When I too am at rest.

But her time of rest was not yet come, and she lived for
seventeen years after her husband.　She was very brave,
she did not turn from the sympathy of her friends, she
endured her loneliness with courage, she worked to dis-
tract her mind.　Here is a touching letter addressed to
Mrs. Taylor, of Norwich, in which she says :—' A thousand
thanks for your kind letter, still more for the very short
visit that preceded it.　Though short — too short —

it has left indelible impressions on my mind. My
heart has truly had communion with yours ; your
sympathy has been balm to it ; and I feel that there is
*now* no one on earth to whom I could pour out that heart
more readily. . . . I am now sitting alone again, and feel
like a person who has been sitting by a cheerful fire, not
sensible at the time of the temperature of the air ; but
the fire removed, he finds the season is still winter. Day
after day passes, and I do not know what to do with my
time ; my mind has no energy nor power of application.'

How much she felt her loneliness appears again and
again from one passage and another. Then she struggled
against discouragement ; she took to her pen again. To
Mrs. Kenrick she writes :—' I intend to pay my letter
debts ; not much troubling my head whether I have anything to say or not ; yet to you my heart has always
something to say : it always recognises you as among the
dearest of its friends ; and while it feels that new impressions are made with difficulty and early effaced, retains,
and ever will retain, I trust beyond this world, those of our
early and long-tried affection.'

She set to work again, trying to forget her heavy
trials. It was during the first years of her widowhood
that she published her edition of the British novelists in
some fifty volumes. There is an opening chapter to this

edition upon novels and novel-writing, which is an admirable and most interesting essay upon fiction, beginning from the very earliest times.

In 1811 she wrote her poem on the King's illness, and also the longer poem which provoked such indignant comments at the time. It describes Britain's rise and luxury, warns her of the dangers of her unbounded ambition and unjustifiable wars :—

> Arts, arms, and wealth destroy the fruits they bring;
> Commerce, like beauty, knows no second spring.

Her ingenuous youth from Ontario's shore who visits the ruins of London is one of the many claimants to the honour of having suggested Lord Macaulay's celebrated New Zealander :—

> Pensive and thoughtful shall the wanderers greet
> Each splendid square and still untrodden street,
> Or of some crumbling turret, mined by time,
> The broken stairs with perilous step shall climb,
> Thence stretch their view the wide horizon round,
> By scattered hamlets trace its ancient bound,
> And, choked no more with fleets, fair Thames survey
> Through reeds and sedge pursue his idle way.

It is impossible not to admire the poem, though it is stilted and not to the present taste. The description

of Britain as it now is and as it once was is very
ingenious :—

> Where once Bonduca whirled the scythèd car,
> And the fierce matrons raised the shriek of war,
> Light forms beneath transparent muslin float,
> And tutor'd voices swell the artful note;
> Light-leaved acacias, and the shady plane,
> And spreading cedars grace the woodland reign.

The poem is forgotten now, though it was scouted
at the time and violently attacked, Southey himself falling
upon the poor old lady, and devouring her, spectacles and
all. She felt these attacks very much, and could not be
consoled, though Miss Edgeworth wrote a warm-hearted
letter of indignant sympathy. But Mrs. Barbauld had
something in her too genuine to be crushed, even by sar-
castic criticism. She published no more, but it was after
her poem of ' 1811 ' that she wrote the beautiful ode by
which she is best known and best remembered,—the ode
that Wordsworth used to repeat and say he envied, that
Tennyson has called ' sweet verses,' of which the lines ring
their tender hopeful chime like sweet church bells on a
summer evening.

Madame d'Arblay, in her old age, told Crabb Robinson
that every night she said the verses over to herself as she
went to her rest. To the writer they are almost sacred.

The hand that patiently pointed out to her, one by one, the syllables of Mrs. Barbauld's hymns for children, that tended our childhood, as it had tended our father's, marked these verses one night, when it blessed us for the last time.

> Life, we've been long together,
> Through pleasant and through cloudy weather ;
> 'Tis hard to part when friends are dear ;
> Perhaps 'twill cost a sigh or tear,
> Then steal away, give little warning,
> Choose thine own time.
> Say not good-night, but in some brighter clime, .
> Bid me ' Good morning.'

Mrs. Barbauld was over seventy when she wrote this ode. A poem, called ' Octogenary Reflections,' is also very touching :—

> Say ye, who through this round of eighty years
> Have proved its joys and sorrows, hopes and fears ;
> Say what is life, ye veterans who have trod,
> Step following steps, its flowery thorny road ?
> Enough of good to kindle strong desire ;
> Enough of ill to damp the rising fire ;
> Enough of love and fancy, joy and hope,
> To fan desire and give the passions scope ;
> Enough of disappointment, sorrow, pain,
> To seal the wise man's sentence—' All is vain.'

There is another fragment of hers in which she likens herself to a schoolboy left of all the train, who hears no

sound of wheels to bear him to his father's bosom home.
' Thus I look to the hour when I shall follow those that
are at rest before me.' And then at last the time came
for which she longed. Her brother died, her faithful Mrs.
Kenrick died, and Mrs. Taylor, whom she loved most of
all. She had consented to give up her solitary home to
spend the remaining years of her life in the home of her
adopted son Charles, now married, and a father; but it was
while she was on a little visit to her sister-in-law, Mrs.
Aikin, that the summons came, very swiftly and peacefully, as she sat in her chair one day. Her nephew tran
scribed these, the last lines she ever wrote :—

' Who are you ? '

' Do you not know me ? have you not expected me ? '

' Whither do you carry me ? '

' Come with me and you shall know.'

' The way is dark.'

' It is well trodden.'

' Yes, in the forward track.'

' Come along.'

' Oh ! shall I there see my beloved ones ? Will they welcome me, and will they know me ? Oh, tell me, tell me ; thou
canst tell me.'

' Yes, but thou must come first.'

' Stop a little ; keep thy hand off till thou hast told me.'

' I never wait.'

' Oh ! shall I see the warm sun again in my cold grave ? '

' Nothing is there that can feel the sun.'

E

' Oh, where then ? '

' Come, I say.'

One may acknowledge the great progress which people have made since Mrs. Barbauld's day in the practice of writing prose and poetry, in the art of expressing upon paper the thoughts which are in most people's minds. It is (to use a friend's simile) like playing upon the piano—everybody now learns to play upon the piano, and it is certain that the modest performances of the ladies of Mrs. Barbauld's time would scarcely meet with the attention now, which they then received. But all the same, the stock of true feeling, of real poetry, is not increased by the increased volubility of our pens ; and so when something comes to us that is real, that is complete in pathos or in wisdom, we still acknowledge the gift, and are grateful for it.

# MISS EDGEWORTH.

1767–1849.

'Exceeding wise, fairspoken, and persuading.'—*Hen. VIII.*

## EARLY DAYS.

### I.

FEW authoresses in these days can have enjoyed the
ovations and attentions which seem to have been considered the due of many of the ladies distinguished at the
end of the last century and the beginning of this one.
To read the accounts of the receptions and compliments
which fell to their lot may well fill later and lesser lumin-
aries with envy. Crowds opened to admit them, banquets
spread themselves out before them, lights were lighted up
and flowers were scattered at their feet. Dukes, editors,
prime ministers, waited their convenience on their stair-
cases; whole theatres rose up *en masse* to greet the gifted
creatures of this and that immortal tragedy. The authoresses themselves, to do them justice, seem to have been
very little dazzled by all this excitement. Hannah More
contentedly retires with her maiden sisters to the Parnassus
on the Mendip Hills, where they sew and chat and make

tea, and teach the village children.   Dear Joanna Baillie,
modest and beloved, lives on to peaceful age in her pretty
old house at Hampstead, looking through tree-tops and
sunshine and clouds towards distant London.   ' Out there
where all the storms are,' I heard the children saying
yesterday as they watched the overhanging gloom of smoke
which veils the city of metropolitan thunders and lightning.   Maria Edgeworth's apparitions as a literary lioness
in the rush of London and of Paris society were but inter-
ludes in her existence, and her real life was one of constant exertion and industry spent far away in an Irish
home among her own kindred and occupations and interests.
We may realise what these were when we read that Mr.
Edgeworth had no less than four wives, who all left
children, and that Maria was the eldest daughter of the
whole family.   Besides this, we must also remember that
the father whom she idolised was himself a man of extraordinary powers, brilliant in conversation (so I have been
told), full of animation, of interest, of plans for his country,
his family, for education and literature, for mechanics and
scientific discoveries ; that he was a gentleman widely connected, hospitably inclined, with a large estate and many
tenants to overlook, with correspondence and acquaintances
all over the world ;  and besides all this, with various
schemes in his brain, to be eventually realised by others of

which velocipedes, tramways, and telegraphs were but a
few of the items.

One could imagine that under these circumstances the
hurry and excitement of London life must have sometimes
seemed tranquillity itself compared with the many and
absorbing interests of such a family. What these interests
were may be gathered from the pages of a very interesting memoir from which the writer of this essay has been
allowed to quote. It is a book privately printed and
written for the use of her children by the widow of
Richard Lovell Edgeworth, and is a record, among other
things, of a faithful and most touching friendship between
Maria and her father's wife—' a friendship lasting for over
fifty years, and unbroken by a single cloud of difference
or mistrust.' Mrs. Edgeworth, who was Miss Beaufort
before her marriage, and about the same age as Miss
Edgeworth, unconsciously reveals her own most charming
and unselfish nature as she tells her stepdaughter's story.

When the writer looks back upon her own childhood,
it seems to her that she lived in company with a delightful host of little playmates, bright, busy, clever children,
whose cheerful presence remains more vividly in her mind
than that of many of the real little boys and girls who
used to appear and disappear disconnectedly as children
do in childhood, when friendship and companionship

depend almost entirely upon the convenience of grown-up
people. Now and again came little cousins or friends to
share our games, but day by day, constant and unchanging,
ever to be relied upon, smiled our most lovable and
friendly companions—simple Susan, lame Jervas, Talbot,
the dear Little Merchants, Jem the widow's son with his
arms round old Lightfoot's neck, the generous Ben, with
his whipcord and his useful proverb of ' waste not, want
not '—all of these were there in the window corner waiting our pleasure. After Parents' Assistant, to which
familiar words we attached no meaning whatever, came
Popular Tales in big brown volumes off a shelf in the
lumber-room of an apartment in an old house in Paris,
and as we opened the books, lo! creation widened to our
view. England, Ireland, America, Turkey, the mines of
Golconda, the streets of Bagdad, thieves, travellers,
governesses, natural philosophy, and fashionable life, were
all laid under contribution, and brought interest and
adventure to our humdrum nursery corner. All Mr.
Edgeworth's varied teaching and experience, all his
daughter's genius of observation, came to interest and
delight our play-time, and that of a thousand other little
children in different parts of the world. People justly
praise Miss Edgeworth's admirable stories and novels, but
from prejudice and early association these beloved childish

histories seem unequalled still, and it is chiefly as a writer for children that we venture to consider her here. Some of the stories are indeed little idylls in their way. Walter Scott, who best knew how to write for the young so as to charm grandfathers as well as Hugh Littlejohn, Esq., and all the grandchildren, is said to have wiped his kind eyes as he put down ' Simple Susan.' A child's book, says a reviewer of those days defining in the ' Quarterly Review,' should be ' not merely less dry, less difficult, than a book for grown-up people; but more rich in interest, more true to nature, more exquisite in art, more abundant in every quality that replies to childhood's keener and fresher perception.' Children like facts, they like short vivid sentences that tell the story: as they listen intently, so they read; every word has its value for them. It has been a real surprise to the writer to find, on re-reading some of these descriptions of scenery and adventure which she had not looked at since her childhood, that the details which she had imagined spread over much space are contained in a few sentences at the beginning of a page. These sentences, however, show the true art of the writer.

It would be difficult to imagine anything better suited to the mind of a very young person than these pleasant stories, so complete in themselves, so interesting, so varied.

The description of Jervas's escape from the mine where
the miners had plotted his destruction, almost rises to
poetry in its simple diction.   Lame Jervas has warned his
master of the miners' plot, and showed him the vein of
ore which they have concealed.   The miners have sworn
vengeance against him, and his life is in danger.   His
master helps him to get away, and comes into the room
before daybreak, bidding him rise and put on the clothes
which he has brought.   ' I followed him out of the house
before anybody else was awake, and he took me across the
fields towards the high road.   At this place we waited till
we heard the tinkling of the bells of a team of horses.
" Here comes the waggon," said he, " in which you are to
go.   So fare you well, Jervas.   I shall hear how you go
on ; and I only hope you will serve your next master,
whoever he may be, as faithfully as you have served me."
" I shall never find so good a master," was all I could say
for the soul of me ; I was quite overcome by his goodness
and sorrow at parting with him, as I then thought, for
ever.'   The description of the journey is very pretty.
' The morning clouds began to clear away ; I could see
my master at some distance, and I kept looking after him
as the waggon went on slowly, and he walked fast away
over the fields.'   Then the sun begins to rise.   The
waggoner goes on whistling, but lame Jervas, to whom

the rising sun was a spectacle wholly surprising, starts up, exclaiming in wonder and admiration. The waggoner bursts into a loud laugh. 'Lud a marcy,' says he, 'to hear un' and look at un' a body would think the oaf had never seen the sun rise afore;' upon which Jervas remembers that he is still in Cornwall, and must not betray himself, and prudently hides behind some parcels, only just in time, for they meet a party of miners, and he hears his enemies' voice hailing the waggoner. All the rest of the day he sits within, and amuses himself by listening to the bells of the team, which jingle continually. 'On our second day's journey, however, I ventured out of my hiding-place. I walked with the waggoner up and down the hills, enjoying the fresh air, the singing of the birds, and the delightful smell of the honeysuckles and the dog-roses in the hedges. All the wild flowers and even the weeds on the banks by the wayside were to me matters of wonder and admiration. At almost every step I paused to observe something that was new to me, and I could not help feeling surprised at the insensibility of my fellow-traveller, who plodded along, and seldom interrupted his whistling except to cry 'Gee, Blackbird, aw woa,' or 'How now, Smiler?' Then Jervas is lost in admiration before a plant 'whose stem was about two feet high, and which had a round shining purple beautiful

flower,' and the waggoner with a look of scorn exclaims,
' Help thee, lad, dost not thou know 'tis a common thistle ? '
After' this he looks upon Jervas as very nearly an idiot.
' In truth I believe I was a droll figure, for my hat was
stuck full of weeds and of all sorts of wild flowers, and
both my coat and waistcoat pockets were stuffed out with
pebbles and funguses.'    Then comes Plymouth Harbour :
Jervas ventures to ask some questions about the vessels, to
which the waggoner answers ' They be nothing in life but
the boats and ships, man ; ' so he turned away and went
on chewing a straw, and seemed not a whit more moved
to admiration than he had been at the sight of the thistle.
' I conceived a high admiration of a man who had seen so
much that he could admire nothing,' says Jervas, with a
touch of real humour.

Another most charming little idyll is that of Simple
Susan, who was a real maiden living in the neighbourhood
of Edgeworthstown.    The story seems to have been mislaid
for a time in the stirring events of the first Irish rebellion,
and overlooked, like some little daisy by a battlefield.
Few among us will not have shared Mr. Edgeworth's parti-
ality for the charming little tale.    The children fling their
garlands and tie up their violets.    Susan bakes her cottage
loaves and gathers marigolds for broth, and tends her
mother to the distant tune of Philip's pipe coming across

the fields.  As we read the story again it seems as if we could almost scent the fragrance of the primroses and the double violets, and hear the music sounding above the children's voices, and the bleatings of the lamb, so simply and delightfully is the whole story constructed.  Among all Miss Edgeworth's characters few are more familiar to the world than that of Susan's pretty pet lamb.


## II.

No sketch of Maria Edgeworth's life, however slight, would be complete without a few words about certain persons coming a generation before her (and belonging still to the age of periwigs), who were her father's associates and her own earliest friends.  Notwithstanding all that has been said of Mr. Edgeworth's bewildering versatility of nature, he seems to have been singularly faithful in his friendships.  He might take up new ties, but he clung pertinaciously to those which had once existed.  His daughter inherited that same steadiness of affection.  In his life of Erasmus Darwin, his grandfather, Mr. Charles Darwin, writing of these very people, has said, 'There is, perhaps, no safer test of a man's real character than that of his long-continued friendship with good and able men.'  He then goes on to quote an instance of a long-continued affection

and intimacy only broken by death between a certain set
of distinguished friends, giving the names of Keir, Day,
Small, Boulton, Watt, Wedgwood, and Darwin, and adding
to them the names of Edgeworth himself and of the Gal-
tons.

Mr. Edgeworth first came to Lichfield to make Dr.
Darwin's acquaintance. His second visit was to his friend
Mr. Day, the author of ' Sandford and Merton,' who had
taken a house in the valley of Stow, and who invited him
one Christmas on a visit. ' About the year 1765,' says Miss
Seward, ' came to Lichfield, from the neighbourhood of
Reading, the young and gay philosopher, Mr. Edgeworth ;
a man of fortune, and recently married to a Miss Elers, of
Oxfordshire. The fame of Dr. Darwin's various talents
allured Mr. E. to the city they graced.' And the lady goes
on to describe Mr. Edgeworth himself:—' Scarcely two-
and-twenty, with an exterior yet more juvenile, having
mathematic science, mechanic ingenuity, and a competent
portion of classical learning, with the possession of the
modern languages. . . . He danced, he fenced, he winged
his arrows with more than philosophic skill,' continues the
lady, herself a person of no little celebrity in her time and
place. Mr. Edgeworth, in his Memoirs, pays a respectful
tribute to Miss Seward's charms, to her agreeable conversation, her beauty, her flowing tresses, her sprightliness and

address. Such moderate expressions fail, however, to do
justice to this lady's powers, to her enthusiasm, her poetry,
her partisanship.  The portrait prefixed to her letters is
that of a dignified person with an oval face and dark eyes,
the thick brown tresses are twined with pearls, her graceful
figure is robed in the softest furs and draperies of the
period.  In her very first letter she thus poetically describes
her surroundings :—' The autumnal glory of this day puts
to shame the summer's sullenness.  I sit writing upon this
dear green terrace, feeding at intervals my little golden-
breasted songsters.  The embosomed vale of Stow glows
sunny through the Claude-Lorraine tint which is spread
over the scene like the blue mist over a plum.'

In this Claude-Lorraine-plum-tinted valley stood the
house which Mr. Day had taken, and where Mr. Edgeworth
had come on an eventful visit.  Miss Seward herself lived
with her parents in the Bishop's palace at Lichfield. There
was also a younger sister, ' Miss Sally,' who died as a girl,
and another very beautiful young lady their friend, by name
Honora Sneyd, placed under Mrs. Seward's care.  She was
the heroine of Major André's unhappy romance.  He too
lived at Lichfield with his mother, and his hopeless love
gives a tragic reality to this by-gone holiday of youth and
merry-making.  As one reads the old letters and memoirs
the echoes of laughter reach us.  One can almost see the

young folks all coming together out of the Cathedral Close, where so much of their time was passed; the beautiful Honora, surrounded by friends and adorers, chaperoned by the graceful Muse her senior, also much admired, and much made of. Thomas Day is perhaps striding after them in silence with keen critical glances; his long black locks flow unpowdered down his back. In contrast to him comes his brilliant and dressy companion, Mr. Edgeworth, who talks so agreeably. I can imagine little Sabrina, Day's adopted foundling, of whom so many stories have been told, following shyly at her guardian's side in her simple dress and childish beauty, and André's young handsome face turned towards Miss Sneyd. So they pass on happy and contented in each other's company, Honora in the midst, beautiful, stately, reserved : she too was one of those not destined to be old.

Miss Seward seems to have loved this friend with a very sincere and admiring affection, and to have bitterly mourned her early death. Her letters abound in apostrophes to the lost Honora. But perhaps the poor Muse expected almost too much from friendship, too much from life. She expected, as we all do at times, that her friends should be not themselves but her, that they should lead not their lives but her own. So much at least one may gather from the various phases of her style and correspondence, and her complaints of Honora's estrangement and subsequent coldness. Perhaps, also, Miss Seward's many vagaries and sentiments may have frozen Honora's sympathies. Miss Seward was all asterisks and notes of exclamation. Honora seems to have forced feeling down to its most scrupulous expression. She never lived to be softened by experience, to suit herself to others by degrees: with great love she also inspired awe and a sort of surprise. One can imagine her pointing the moral of the purple jar, as it was told long afterwards by her stepdaughter, then a little girl playing at her own mother's knee in her nursery by the river.

People in the days of shilling postage were better correspondents than they are now when we have to be content with pennyworths of news and of affectionate intercourse. Their descriptions and many details bring all the chief characters vividly before us, and carry us into the hearts and the pocket-books of the little society at Lichfield as it then was. The town must have been an agreeable sojourn in those days for people of some pretension and small performance. The inhabitants of Lichfield seem actually to have read each other's verses, and having done so to have taken the trouble to sit down and write out their raptures. They were a pleasant lively company living round about the old cathedral towers, meeting in the

Close or the adjacent gardens or the hospitable Palace itself. Here the company would sip tea, talk mild literature of their own and good criticism at second hand, quoting Dr. Johnson to one another with the familiarity of townsfolk. From Erasmus Darwin, too, they must have gained something of vigour and originality.

With all her absurdities Miss Seward had some real critical power and appreciation ; and some of her lines are very pretty.[1] An ' Ode to the Sun ' is only what might have been expected from this Lichfield Corinne. Her best known productions are an ' Elegy on Captain Cook,' a ' Monody on Major André,' whom she had known from her early youth ; and there is a poem, ' Louisa,' of which she herself speaks very highly. But even more than her poetry did she pique herself upon her epistolary correspondence. It must have been well worth while writing letters when they were not only prized by the writer and the recipients, but commented on by their friends in after years. ' Court Dewes, Esq.,' writes, after

---

In a notice of Miss Seward in the *Annual Register*, just after her death in 1809, the writer, who seems to have known her, says :—' Conscious of ability, she freely displayed herself in a manner equally remote from annoyance and affectation. . . . . Her errors arose from a glowing imagination joined to an excessive sensibility, cherished instead of repressed by early habits. It is understood that she has left the whole of her works to Mr. Scott, the northern poet, with a view to their publication with her life and posthumous pieces.'

five years, for copies of Miss Seward's epistles to Miss
Rogers and Miss Weston, of which the latter begins :—
' Soothing and welcome to me, dear Sophia, is the regret
you express for our separation ! Pleasant were the weeks
we have recently passed together in this ancient and em-
bowered mansion ! I had strongly felt the silence and
vacancy of the depriving day on which you vanished.
How prone are our hearts perversely to quarrel with the
friendly coercion of employment at the very instant in
which it is clearing the torpid and injurious mists of un-
availing melancholy!' Then follows a sprightly attack
before which Johnson may have quailed indeed. ' Is the
Fe-fa-fum of literature that snuffs afar the fame of his
brother authors, and thirsts for its destruction, to be
allowed to gallop unmolested over the fields of criticism ?
A few pebbles from the well-springs of truth and eloquence are all that is wanted to bring the might of his
envy low.' This celebrated letter, which may stand as
a specimen of the whole six volumes, concludes with the
following apostrophe :—'Virtuous friendship, how pure, how
sacred are thy delights ! Sophia, thy mind is capable of
tasting them in all their poignance : against how many of
life's incidents may that capacity be considered as a
counterpoise !'

There were constant rubs, which are not to be

F

wondered at, between Miss Seward and Dr. Darwin, who, though a poet, was also a singularly witty, downright man, outspoken and humorous. The lady admires his genius, bitterly resents his sarcasms; of his celebrated work, the ' Botanic Garden,' she says, ' It is a string of poetic brilliants, and they are of the first water, but the eye will be apt to want the intersticial black velvet to give effect to their lustre.' In later days, notwithstanding her ' elegant language,' as Mr. Charles Darwin calls it, she said several spiteful things of her old friend, but they seem more prompted by private pique than malice.

If Miss Seward was the Minerva and Dr. Darwin the Jupiter of the Lichfield society, its philosopher was Thomas Day, of whom Miss Seward's description is so good that I cannot help one more quotation :—

' Powder and fine clothes were at that time the appendages of gentlemen ; Mr. Day wore not either. He was tall and stooped in the shoulders, full made but not corpulent, and in his meditative and melancholy air a degree of awkwardness and dignity were blended.' She then compares him with his guest, Mr. Edgeworth. ' Less graceful, less amusing, less brilliant than Mr. E., but more highly imaginative, more classical, and a deeper reasoner ; strict integrity, energetic friendship, open-handed generosity, and diffusive charity, greatly overbalanced on the side of virtue, the tincture of misanthropic gloom and proud contempt of common life society.' Wright, of Derby, painted a full-length picture of Mr. Day in 1770. ' Mr. Day looks upward enthusiastically, meditating on the contents of a book held in his dropped right hand . . . a flash of lightning plays in his hair and illuminates the contents of the volume.' ' Dr. Darwin,' adds Miss Seward, ' sat to Mr. Wright about the same period—*that* was a simply contemplative portrait of the most perfect resemblance.'

## III.

Maria must have been three years old this eventful Christmas time when her father, leaving his wife in Berkshire, came to stay with Mr. Day at Lichfield, and first made the acquaintance of Miss Seward and her poetic circle. Mr. Day, who had once already been disappointed in love, and whose romantic scheme of adopting his foundlings and of educating one of them to be his wife, has often been described, had brought one of the maidens to the house he had taken at Lichfield. This was Sabrina, as he had called her. Lucretia, having been found troublesome, had been sent off with a dowry to be apprenticed to a milliner. Sabrina was a charming little girl of thirteen ; everybody liked her, especially the friendly ladies at the

Palace, who received her with constant kindness, as they did Mr. Day himself and his visitor. What Miss Seward thought of Sabrina's education I do not know. The poor child was to be taught to despise luxury, to ignore fear, to be superior to pain. She appears, however, to have been very fond of her benefactor, but to have constantly provoked him by starting and screaming whenever he fired uncharged pistols at her skirts, or dropped hot melted sealing-wax on her bare arms. She is described as lovely and artless, not fond of books, incapable of understanding scientific problems, or of keeping the imaginary and terrible secrets with which her guardian used to try her nerves. I do not know when it first occurred to him that Honora Sneyd was all that his dreams could have imagined. One day he left Sabrina under many restrictions, and returning unexpectedly found her wearing some garment or handkerchief of which he did not approve, and discarded her on the spot and for ever. Poor Sabrina was evidently not meant to mate and soar with philosophical eagles. After this episode, she too was despatched, to board with an old lady, in peace for a time, let us hope, and in tranquil mediocrity.

Mr. Edgeworth approved of this arrangement ; he had never considered that Sabrina was suited to his friend. But being taken in due time to call at the Palace, he was charmed with Miss Seward, and still more by all he saw of Honora ; comparing her, alas! in his mind 'with all other women, and secretly acknowledging her superiority.' At first, he says, Miss Seward's brilliance overshadowed Honora, but very soon her merits grew upon the bystanders.

Mr. Edgeworth carefully concealed his feelings except from his host, who was beginning himself to contemplate a marriage with Miss Sneyd. Mr. Day presently proposed formally in writing for the hand of the lovely Honora, and Mr. Edgeworth was to take the packet and to bring back the answer ; and being married himself, and out of the running, he appears to have been unselfishly anxious for his friend's success. In the packet Mr. Day had written down the conditions to which he should expect his wife to subscribe. She would have to begin at once by giving up all luxuries, amenities, and intercourse with the world, and promise to continue to seclude herself entirely in his company. Miss Sneyd does not seem to have kept Mr. Edgeworth waiting long while she wrote her answer decidedly saying that she could not admit the unqualified control of a husband over all her actions, nor the necessity for ' seclusion from society to preserve female virtue.' Finding that Honora absolutely refused to change her way of life, Mr. Day went into a fever, for which Dr. Darwin bled him. Nor did he recover until another Miss Sneyd, Elizabeth by name, made her appearance in the Close.

Mr. Edgeworth, who was of a lively and active disposition, had introduced archery among the gentlemen of the neighbourhood, and he describes a fine summer evening's entertainment passed in agreeable sports, followed by dancing and music, in the course of which Honora's sister, Miss Elizabeth, appeared for the first time on the Lichfield scene, and immediately joined in the country dance. There is a vivid description of the two sisters in Mr. Edgeworth's memoirs, of the beautiful and distinguished Honora, loving science, serious, eager, reserved; of the more lovely but less graceful Elizabeth, with less of energy, more of humour and of social gifts than her sister. Elizabeth Sneyd was, says Edgeworth, struck by Day's eloquence, by his unbounded generosity, by his scorn of wealth. His educating a young girl for his wife seemed to her romantic and extraordinary; and she seems to have thought it possible to yield to the evident admiration she had aroused in him. But, whether in fun or in seriousness, she represented to him that he could not with justice decry accomplishments and graces that he had not acquired. She wished him to go abroad for a time to study to perfect himself in all that was wanting; on her own part she promised not to go to Bath, London, or any public place of amusement until his return, and to read certain books which he recommended.

Meanwhile Mr. Edgeworth had made no secret of his own feeling for Honora to Mr. Day, 'who with all the eloquence of virtue and of friendship' urged him to fly, to accompany him abroad, and to shun dangers he could not hope to overcome. Edgeworth consented to this proposal, and the two friends started for Paris, visiting Rousseau on their way. They spent the winter at Lyons, as it was a place where excellent masters of all sorts were to be found ; and here Mr. Day, with excess of zeal—

put himself (says his friend) to every species of torture, ordinary and extraordinary, to compel his Antigallican limbs, in spite of their natural rigidity, to dance and fence, and manage the *great horse*. To perform his promise to Miss E. Sneyd honourably, he gave up seven or eight hours of the day to these exercises, for which he had not the slightest taste, and for which, except horsemanship, he manifested the most sovereign contempt. It was astonishing to behold the energy with which he persevered in these pursuits. I have seen him stand between two boards which reached from the ground higher than his knees : these boards were adjusted with screws so as barely to permit him to bend his knees, and to rise up and sink down. By these means Mr. Huise proposed to force Mr. Day's knees outwards ; but screwing was in vain. He succeeded in torturing his patient ; but original formation and inveterate habit resisted all his endeavours at personal improvement. I could not help pitying my philosophic friend, pent up in durance vile for hours together, with his feet in the stocks, a book in his hand, and contempt in his heart.

Mr. Edgeworth meanwhile lodged himself 'in excellent

and agreeable apartments,' and occupied himself with engineering. He is certainly curiously outspoken in his memoirs; and explains that the first Mrs. Edgeworth, Maria's mother, with many merits, was of a complaining disposition, and did not make him so happy at home as a woman of a more lively temper might have succeeded in doing. He was tempted, he said, to look for happiness elsewhere than in his home. Perhaps domestic affairs may have been complicated by a warm-hearted but troublesome little son, who at Day's suggestion had been brought up upon the Rousseau system, and was in consequence quite unmanageable, and a worry to everybody. Poor Mrs. Edgeworth's complainings were not to last very long. She joined her husband at Lyons, and after a time, having a dread of lying in abroad, returned home to die in her confinement, leaving four little children. Maria could remember being taken into her mother's room to see her for the last time.

Mr. Edgeworth hurried back to England, and was met by his friend Thomas Day, who had preceded him, and whose own suit does not seem to have prospered meanwhile. But though notwithstanding all his efforts Thomas Day had not been fortunate in securing Elizabeth Sneyd's affections, he could still feel for his friend. His first words were to tell Edgeworth that Honora was still free, more beautiful than ever; while Virtue and Honour commanded it, he had done all he could to divide them; now he wished to be the first to promote their meeting. The meeting resulted in an engagement, and Mr. Edgeworth and Miss Sneyd were married within four months by the benevolent old canon in the Lady Chapel of Lichfield Cathedral.

Mrs. Seward wept; Miss Seward, 'notwithstanding some imaginary dissatisfaction about a bridesmaid,' was really glad of the marriage, we are told; and the young couple immediately went over to Ireland.

## IV.

Though her life was so short, Honora Edgeworth seems to have made the deepest impression on all those she came across. Over little Maria she had the greatest influence. There is a pretty description of the child standing lost in wondering admiration of her stepmother's beauty, as she watched her soon after her marriage dressing at her toilet-table. Little Maria's feeling for her stepmother was very deep and real, and the influence of those few years lasted for a lifetime. Her own exquisite careful-ness she always ascribed to it, and to this example may also be attributed her habits of order and self-government, her life of reason and deliberate judgment.

The seven years of Honora's married life seem to have been very peaceful and happy. She shared her husband's pursuits, and wished for nothing outside her own home. She began with him to write those little books which were afterwards published. It is just a century ago since she and Mr. Edgeworth planned the early histories of Harry and Lucy and Frank ; while Mr. Day began his ' Sandford and Merton,' which at first was intended to appear at the same time, though eventually the third part was not published till 1789.

As a girl of seventeen Honora Sneyd had once been threatened with consumption. After seven years of married life the cruel malady again declared itself ; and though Dr. Darwin did all that human resource could do, and though every tender care surrounded her, the poor young lady rapidly sank. There is a sad, prim, most affecting letter, addressed to little Maria by the dying woman shortly before the end ; and then comes that one written by the father, which is to tell her that all is over.

If Mr. Edgeworth was certainly unfortunate in losing again and again the happiness of his home, he was more fortunate than most people in being able to rally from his grief. He does not appear to have been unfaithful in feeling. Years after, Edgeworth, writing to console Mrs. Day upon her husband's death, speaks in the most touching way of all he had suffered when Honora died, and of the struggle he had made to regain his hold of life. This letter is in curious contrast to that one written at the time, as he sits by poor Honora's deathbed; it reads strangely cold and irrelevant in these days when people are not ashamed of feeling or of describing what they feel. 'Continue, my dear daughter'—he writes to Maria, who was then thirteen years old—' the desire which you feel of becoming amiable, prudent, and of use. The ornamental parts of a character, with such an understanding as yours, necessarily ensue ; but true judgment and sagacity in the choice of friends, and the regulation of your behaviour, can be only had from reflection, and from being thoroughly convinced of what experience in general teaches too late, that to be happy we must be good.'

' Such a letter, written at such a time,' says the kind biographer, 'made the impression it was intended to convey ; and the wish to act up to the high opinion her father had formed of her character became an exciting and controlling power over the whole of Maria's future life.' On her deathbed, Honora urged her husband to marry again, and assured him that the woman to suit him was her sister Elizabeth. Her influence was so great upon them both that, although Elizabeth was attached to some one else, and Mr. Edgeworth believed her to be little suited to himself, they were presently engaged and married, not without many difficulties. The result proved how rightly Honora had judged.

It was to her father hat Maria owed the suggestion of her first start in literature. Immediately after Honora's death he tells her to write a tale about the length of a 'Spectator,' on the subject of generosity. 'It must be taken from history or romance, must be sent the day se'nnight after you receive this; and I beg you will take some pains about it.' A young gentleman from Oxford was also set to work to try his powers on the same subject, and Mr. William Sneyd, at Lichfield, was to be judge between the two performances. He gave his verdict for Maria: 'An excellent story and very well written: but where's the generosity?' This, we are told, became a sort of proverb in the Edgeworth family.

The little girl meanwhile had been sent to school to a certain Mrs. Lataffiere, where she was taught to use her fingers, to write a lovely delicate hand, to work white satin waistcoats for her papa. She was then removed to a fashionable establishment in Upper Wimpole Street, where, says her stepmother, 'she underwent all the usual tortures of backboards, iron collars, and dumb-bells, with the unusual one of being hung by the neck to draw out the muscles and increase the growth,—a signal failure in her case.' (Miss

Edgeworth was always a very tiny person.) There is a description given of Maria at this school of hers of the little maiden absorbed in her book with all the other children at play, while she sits in her favourite place in front of a carved oak cabinet, quite unconscious of the presence of the romping girls all about her.

Hers was a very interesting character as it appears in the Memoirs—sincere, intelligent, self-contained, and yet dependent; methodical, observant. Sometimes as one reads of her in early life one is reminded of some of the personal characteristics of the writer who perhaps of all writers least resembles Miss Edgeworth in her art—of Charlotte Brontë, whose books are essentially of the modern and passionate school, but whose strangely mixed character seemed rather to belong to the orderly and neatly ruled existence of Queen Charlotte's reign. People's lives as they really are don't perhaps vary very much, but people's lives as they seem to be assuredly change with the fashions. Miss Edgeworth and Miss Bronte were both Irishwomen, who have often, with all their outcome, the timidity which arises from quick and sensitive feeling. But the likeness does not go very deep. Maria, whose diffidence and timidity were personal, but who had a firm and unalterable belief in family traditions, may have been saved from some danger of prejudice and limitation by a most fortunate though trying illness which affected her eyesight, and which caused her to be removed from her school with its monstrous elegancies to the care of Mr. Day, that kindest and sternest of friends.

This philosopher in love had been bitterly mortified when the lively Elizabeth Sneyd, instead of welcoming his return, could not conceal her laughter at his uncouth elegancies, and confessed that, on the whole, she had liked him better as he was before. He forswore Lichfield and marriage, and went abroad to forget. He turned his thoughts to politics; he wrote pamphlets on public subjects and letters upon slavery. His poem of the 'Dying Negro' had been very much admired. Miss Hannah More speaks of it in her Memoirs. The subject of slavery was much before people's minds, and Day's influence had not a little to do with the rising indignation.

Among Day's readers and admirers was one person who was destined to have a most important influence upon his life. By a strange chance his extraordinary ideal was destined to be realised; and a young lady, good, accomplished, rich, devoted, who had read his books, and sympathised with his generous dreams, was ready not only to consent to his strange conditions, but to give him her whole heart and find her best happiness in his society and

in carrying out his experiments and fancies. She was Miss
Esther Milnes, of Yorkshire, an heiress; and though at
first Day hesitated and could not believe in the reality of
her feeling, her constancy and singleness of mind were not
to be resisted, and they were married at Bath in 1778.
We hear of Mr. and Mrs. Day spending the first winter
of their married life at Hampstead, and of Mrs. Day,
thickly shodden, walking with him in a snowstorm on the
common, and ascribing her renewed vigour to her husband's
Spartan advice.

Day and his wife eventually established themselves at
Anningsley, near Chobham. He had insisted upon settling
her fortune upon herself, but Mrs. Day assisted him in
every way, and sympathised in his many schemes and
benevolent ventures. When he neglected to make a
window to the dressing-room he built for her, we hear of her
uncomplainingly lighting her candles; to please him she
worked as a servant in the house, and all their large means
were bestowed in philanthropic and charitable schemes.
Mr. Edgeworth quotes his friend's reproof to Mrs. Day,
who was fond of music: 'Shall we beguile the time with
the strains of a lute while our fellow-creatures are
starving?' 'I am out of pocket every year about 300*l.*
by the farm I keep,' Day writes his to his friend Edgeworth.
'The soil I have taken in hand, I am convinced, is one of

the most completely barren in England.' He then goes
on to explain his reasons for what he is about. 'It enables
me to employ the poor, and the result of all my specula-
tions about humanity is that the only way of benefiting
mankind is to give them employment and make them earn
their money.' There is a pretty description of the worthy
couple in their home dispensing help and benefits all
round about, draining, planting, teaching, doctoring—
nothing came amiss to them. Their chief friend and
neighbour was Samuel Cobbett, who understood their
plans, and sympathised in their efforts, which, naturally
enough, were viewed with doubt and mistrust by most of
the people round about. It was at Anningsley that Mr.
Day finished 'Sandford and Merton,' begun many years
before. His death was very sudden, and was brought about
by one of his own benevolent theories. He used to main-
tain that kindness alone could tame animals; and he was
killed by a fall from a favourite colt which he was breaking
in. Mrs. Day never recovered the shock. She lived two
years hidden in her home, absolutely inconsolable, and
then died and was laid by her husband's side in the churchyard at Wargrave by the river.

It was to the care of these worthy people that little
Maria was sent when she was ill, and she was doctored by
them both physically and morally. 'Bishop Berkeley's

tar-water was still considered a specific for all complaints,'
says Mrs. Edgeworth. ' Mr. Day thought it would be of
use to Maria's inflamed eyes, and he used to bring a large
tumbler full of it to her every morning. She dreaded his
" Now, Miss Maria, drink this." But there was, in spite of
his stern voice, something of pity and sympathy in his
countenance. His excellent library was open to her, and
he directed her studies. His severe reasoning and uncompromising truth of mind awakened all her powers, and the
questions he put to her and the working out of the
answers, the necessity of perfect accuracy in all her words,
suited the natural truth of her mind; and though such
strictness was not agreeable, she even then perceived its
advantage, and in after life was grateful for it.'


## V.

We have seen how Miss Elizabeth Sneyd, who could
not make up her mind to marry Mr. Day notwithstanding
all he had gone through for her sake, had eventually consented to become Mr. Edgeworth's third wife. With this
stepmother for many years to come Maria lived in an
affectionate intimacy, only to be exceeded by that most
faithful companionship which existed for fifty years between her and the lady from whose memoirs I quote.

It was about 1782 that Maria went home to live at Edgeworthtown with her father and his wife, with the many young brothers and sisters. The family was a large one, and already consisted of her own sisters, of Honora the daughter of Mrs. Honora, and Lovell her son. To these succeeded many others of the third generation; and two sisters of Mrs. Edgeworth's, who also made their home at Edgeworthtown.

Maria had once before been there, very young, but she was now old enough to be struck with the difference then so striking between Ireland and England. The tones and looks, the melancholy and the gaiety of the people, were so new and extraordinary to her that the delineations she long afterwards made of Irish character probably owe their life and truth to the impression made on her mind at this time as a stranger. Though it was June when they landed, there was snow on the roses she ran out to gather, and she felt altogether in a new and unfamiliar country.

She herself describes the feelings of the master of a family returning to an Irish home :—

Wherever he turned his eyes, in or out of his home, damp dilapidation, waste appeared. Painting, glazing, roofing, fencing, finishing—all were wanting. The backyard and even the front lawn round the windows of the house were filled with loungers, followers, and petitioners; tenants, undertenants, drivers, sub-agent and agent were to have audience; and they all had grievances and secret informations, accusations, reciprocations, and quarrels each under each interminable.

Her account of her father's dealings with them is
admirable :—

I was with him constantly, and I was amused and interested
in seeing how he made his way through their complaints,
petitions, and grievances with decision and despatch, he all the
time in good humour with the people and they delighted with
him, though he often rated them roundly when they stood before
him perverse in litigation, helpless in procrastination, detected
in cunning or convicted of falsehood. They saw into his
character almost as soon as he understood theirs.

Mr. Edgeworth had in a very remarkable degree that
power of ruling and administering which is one of the
rarest of gifts. He seems to have shown great firmness and
good sense in his conduct in the troubled times in which
he lived. He saw to his own affairs, administered justice,
put down middlemen as far as possible, reorganised the
letting out of the estate. Unlike many of his neighbours,
he was careful not to sacrifice the future to present ease of
mind and of pocket. He put down rack-rents and bribes
of every sort, and did his best to establish things upon a
firm and lasting basis.

But if it was not possible even for Mr. Edgeworth to make
such things all they should have been outside the house,
the sketch given of the family life at home is very pleasant.
The father lives in perfect confidence with his children,
admitting them to his confidence, interesting them in his

experiments, spending his days with them, consulting them. There are no reservations; he does his business in the great sitting-room, surrounded by his family. I have heard it described as a large ground-floor room, with windows to the garden and with two columns supporting the further end, by one of which Maria's writing-desk used to be placed—a desk which her father had devised for her, which used to be drawn out to the fireside when she worked. Does not Mr. Edgeworth also mention in one of his letters a picture of Thomas Day hanging over a sofa against the wall? Books in plenty there were, we may be sure, and perhaps models of ingenious machines and different appliances for scientific work. Sir Henry Holland and Mr. Ticknor give a curious description of Mr. Edgeworth's many ingenious inventions. There were strange locks to the rooms and telegraphic despatches to the kitchen; clocks at the one side of the house were wound up by simply opening certain doors at the other end. It has been remarked that all Miss Edgeworth's heroes had a smattering of science. Several of her brothers inherited her father's turn for it. We hear of them raising steeples and establishing telegraphs in partnership with him. Maria shared of the family labours and used to help her father in the business connected with the estate, to assist him, also, to keep the accounts. She had a special turn for accounts, and she was pleased with her exquisitely neat columns and by the accuracy with which her figures fell into their proper places. Long after her father's death this knowledge and experience enabled her to manage the estate for her eldest stepbrother, Mr. Lovell Edgeworth. She was able, at a time of great national difficulty and anxious crisis, to meet a storm in which many a larger fortune was wrecked.

But in 1782 she was a young girl only beginning life. Storms were not yet, and she was putting out her wings in the sunshine. Her father set her to translate ' Adèle et Théodore,' by Madame de Genlis (she had a great facility for languages, and her French was really remarkable). Holcroft's version of the book, however, appeared, and the Edgeworth translation was never completed. Mr. Day wrote a letter to congratulate Mr. Edgeworth on the occasion. It seemed horrible to Mr. Day that a woman should appear in print.

It is possible that the Edgeworth family was no exception to the rule by which large and clever and animated families are apt to live in a certain atmosphere of their own. But, notwithstanding this strong family bias, few people can have seen more of the world, felt its temper more justly, or appreciated more fully the interesting varieties of people to be found in it than Maria Edgeworth. Within easy reach of Edgeworthtown were different agreeable and cultivated houses. There was Pakenham Hall with Lord Longford for its master; one of its daughters was the future Duchess of Wellington, 'who was always Kitty Pakenham for her old friends.' There at Castle Forbes also lived, I take it, more than one of the well-bred and delightful persons, out of 'Patronage,' and the 'Absentee,' who may, in real life, have borne the names of Lady Moira and Lady Granard. Besides, there were cousins and relations without number—Foxes, Ruxtons, marriages and intermarriages; and when the time came for occasional absences and expeditions from home, the circles seem to have spread incalculably in every direction. The Edgeworths appear to have been a genuinely sociable clan, interested in others and certainly interesting to them.

## VI.

The first letter given in the Memoirs from Maria to her favourite aunt Ruxton is a very sad one, which tells of the early death of her sister Honora, a beautiful girl of fifteen, the only daughter of Mrs. Honora Edgeworth, who died of consumption, as her mother had died. This letter, written in the dry phraseology of the time, is nevertheless full of feeling, above all for her father who was, as Maria says elsewhere, ever since she could think or feel, the first object and motive of her mind.

Mrs. Edgeworth describes her sister-in-law as follows:—

Mrs. Ruxton resembled her brother in the wit and vivacity of her mind and strong affections; her grace and charm of manner were such that a gentleman once said of her; 'If I were to see Mrs. Ruxton in rags as a beggar woman sitting on the doorstep, I should say "Madam" to her.' 'To write to her Aunt Ruxton was, as long as she lived, Maria's greatest pleasure while away from her,' says Mrs. Edgeworth, 'and to be with her was a happiness she enjoyed with never flagging and supreme delight. Blackcastle was within a few hours' drive of Edgeworthtown, and to go to Blackcastle was the holiday of her life.

Mrs. Edgeworth tells a story of Maria once staying at Blackcastle and tearing out the title page of 'Belinda,' so that her aunt, Mrs. Ruxton, read the book without any suspicion of the author. She was so delighted with it that she insisted on Maria listening to page after page, exclaiming 'Is not that admirably written?' 'Admirably read, I think,' said Maria; until her aunt, quite provoked by her faint acquiescence, says, 'I am sorry to see my little Maria unable to bear the praises of a rival author;' at which poor Maria burst into tears, and Mrs. Ruxton could never bear the book mentioned afterwards.

It was with Mrs. Ruxton that a little boy, born just after the death of the author of 'Sandford and Merton,'

was left on the occasion of the departure of the Edgeworth
family for Clifton, in 1792, where Mr. Edgeworth spent a
couple of years for the health of one of his sons.    In July
the poor little brother dies in Ireland.    ' There does
not, now that little Thomas is gone, exist even a person
of the same name as Mr. Day,' says Mr. Edgeworth,
who concludes his letter philosophically, as the father of
twenty children may be allowed to do, by expressing a
hope that to his nurses, Mrs. Ruxton and her daughter,
' the remembrance of their own goodness will soon
obliterate the painful impression of his miserable end.'
During their stay at Clifton Richard Edgeworth, the
eldest son, who had been brought up upon Rousseau's
system, and who seems to have found the Old World too
restricted a sphere for his energies, after going to sea and
disappearing for some years, suddenly paid them a visit
from South Carolina, where he had settled and married.
The young man was gladly welcomed by them all.    He
had been long separated from home, and he eventually
died very young in America; but his sister always clung
to him with fond affection, and when he left them to
return home she seems to have felt his departure very
much.    ' Last Saturday my poor brother Richard took
leave of us to return to America.    He has gone up to
London with my father and mother, and is to sail from

thence.  We could not part from him without great pain and regret, for he made us all extremely fond of him.'

Notwithstanding these melancholy events, Maria Edgeworth seems to have led a happy busy life all this time among her friends, her relations, her many interests, her many fancies and facts, making much of the children, of whom she writes pleasant descriptions to her aunt. 'Charlotte is very engaging and promises to be handsome. Sneyd is, and promises everything.  Henry will, I think, through life always do more than he promises.  Little Honora is a sprightly blue-eyed child at nurse with a woman who is the picture of health and simplicity. Lovell is perfectly well.  Doctor Darwin has paid him very handsome compliments on his lines on the Barbarini Vase in the first part of the "Botanic Garden."'

Mr. Edgeworth, however, found the time long at Clifton, though, as usual, he at once improved his opportunities, paid visits to his friends in London and elsewhere, and renewed many former intimacies and correspondences.

Maria also paid a visit to London, but the time had not come for her to enjoy society, and the extreme shyness of which Mrs. Edgeworth speaks made it pain to her to be in society in those early days.  'Since I have been away from home,' she writes, 'I have missed the society of my father, mother, and sisters more than I can express, and more than beforehand I could have thought possible. I long to see them all again. Even when I am most amused I feel a void, and now I understand what an aching void is perfectly.' Very soon we hear of her at home again, ' scratching away at the Freeman family.' Mr. Edgeworth is reading aloud Gay's ' Trivia ' among other things, which she recommends to her aunt. ' I had much rather make a bargain with any one I loved to read the same books with them at the same hour than to look at the moon like Rousseau's famous lovers.' There is another book, a new book for the children, mentioned about this time, ' Evenings at Home,' which they all admire immensely.

Miss Edgeworth was now about twenty-six, at an age when a woman's powers have fully ripened ; a change comes over her style ; there is a fulness of description in her letters and a security of expression which show maturity. Her habit of writing was now established, and she describes the constant interest her father took and his share in all she did. Some of the slighter stories she first wrote upon a slate and read out to her brothers and sisters ; others she sketched for her father's approval, and arranged and altered as he suggested. The letters for literary ladies were with the publishers by this time, and these were followed by various stories and early lessons, portions of ' Parents '

Assistant,' and of popular tales, all of which were sent out in packets and lent from one member of the family to another before finally reaching Mr. Johnson, the publisher's, hands. Maria Edgeworth in some of her letters from Clifton alludes with some indignation to the story of Mrs. Hannah More's ungrateful *protégée* Lactilla, the literary milkwoman, whose poems Hannah More was at such pains to bring before the world, and for whom, with her kind preface and warm commendations and subscription list, she was able to obtain the large sum of 500*l*. The ungrateful Lactilla, who had been starving when Mrs. More found her out, seems to have lost her head in this sudden prosperity, and to have accused her benefactress of wishing to steal a portion of the money. Maria Edgeworth must have been also interested in some family marriages which took place about this time. Her own sister Anna became engaged to Dr. Beddoes, of Clifton, whose name appears as prescribing for the authors of various memoirs of that day. He is 'a man of ability, of a great name in the scientific world,' says Mr. Edgeworth, who favoured the Doctor's ' declared passion,' as a proposal was then called, and the marriage accordingly took place on their return to Ireland. Emmeline, another sister, was soon after married to Mr. King, a surgeon, also living at Bristol, and Maria was now left the only remaining daughter of the first marriage, to be good aunt, sister, friend to all the younger members of the party. She was all this, but she herself expressly states that her father would never allow her to be turned into a nursery drudge ; her share of the family was limited to one special little boy. Meanwhile her pen-and-ink children are growing up, and starting out in the world on their own merits.

' I beg, dear Sophy,' she writes to her cousin, ' that you will not call my little stories by the sublime name of my works ; I shall else be ashamed when the little mouse comes forth. The stories are printed and bound the same size as ' Evenings at Home,' but I am afraid you will dislike the title. My father had sent the ' Parents' Friend,' but Mr. Johnson has degraded it into ' Parents' Assistant.'

In 1797, says Miss Beaufort, who was to be so soon more intimately connected with the Edgeworth family, Johnson wished to publish more volumes of the ' Parents' Assistant ' on fine paper, with prints, and Mrs. Ruxton asked me to make some designs for them. These designs seem to have given great satisfaction to the Edgeworth party, and especially to a little boy called William, Mrs. Edgeworth's youngest boy, who grew up to be a fine young man, but who died young of the cruel family complaint. Mrs. Edgeworth's health was also failing all this time—'Though she makes epigrams she is far from well,' says Maria; but they, none of them seem seriously alarmed. Mr. Edgeworth, in the intervals of politics, is absorbed in a telegraph, which, with the help of his sons, he is trying to establish. It is one which will act by night as well as by day.

It was a time of change and stir for Ireland, disaffection growing and put down for a time by the soldiers; armed bands going about 'defending' the country and breaking its windows. In 1794 threats of a French invasion had alarmed everybody, and now again in 1796 came rumours of every description, and Mr. Edgeworth was very much disappointed that his proposal for establishing a telegraph across the water to England was rejected by Government. He also writes to Dr. Darwin that he had offered himself as a candidate for the county, and been obliged to relinquish at the last moment; but these minor disappointments were lost in the trouble which fell upon the household in the following year—the death of the mother of the family, who sank rapidly and died of consumption in 1797.

## VII.

When Mr. Edgeworth himself died (not, as we may be sure, without many active post-mortem wishes and directions) he left his entertaining Memoirs half finished, and he desired his daughter Maria in the most emphatic way to complete them, and to publish them without changing or altering anything that he had written. People reading them were surprised by the contents ; many blamed Miss Edgeworth for making them public, not knowing how solemn and binding these dying commands of her father's had been, says Mrs. Leadbeater, writing at the time to Mrs. Trench. Many severe and wounding reviews appeared, and this may have influenced Miss Edgeworth in her own objection to having her Memoirs published by her family.

Mr. Edgeworth's life was most extraordinary, comprising in fact three or four lives in the place of that one usually allowed to most people, some of us having to be moderately content with a half or three-quarters of existence. But his versatility of mind was no less remarkable than his tenacity of purpose and strength of affection, though some measure of sentiment must have certainly been wanting, and his fourth marriage must have taken most people by surprise. The writer once expressed .her surprise at the extraordinary influence that Mr. Edgeworth seems to have had over women and over the many members of his family who continued to reside in his home after all the various changes which had taken place there. Lady S——— to whom she spoke is one who has seen more of life than most of us, who has for years past carried help to the far-away and mysterious East, but whose natural place is at home in the more prosperous and unattainable West End. This lady said, ' You do not in the least understand what my Uncle Edgeworth was. I never knew anything like him. Brilliant, full of energy and charm, he was something quite extraordinary and irresistible. If you had known him you would not have wondered at anything.'

' I had in the spring of that year (1797) paid my first visit to Edgeworthtown with my mother and sister,' writes Miss Beaufort, afterwards Mrs. Edgeworth, the author of the Memoirs. ' My father had long before been there, and had frequently met Mr. Edgeworth at Mrs. Ruxton's. In 1795 my father was presented to the living of Collon, in the county of Louth, where he resided from that time. His vicarage was within five minutes' walk of the residence of Mr. Foster, then Speaker of the Irish House of Commons, the dear friend of Mr. Edgeworth, who came to Collon in the spring of 1798 several times, and at last offered me his hand, which I accepted.'

Maria, who was at first very much opposed to the match,

would not have been herself the most devoted and faithful
of daughters if she had not eventually agreed to her
father's wishes, and, as daughters do, come by degrees to
feel with him and to see with his eyes. The influence of
a father over a daughter where real sympathy exists is one
of the very deepest and strongest that can be imagined.
Miss Beaufort herself seems also to have had some special
attraction for Maria. She was about her own age. She
must have been a person of singularly sweet character and
gentle liberality of mind. 'You will come into a new
family, but you will not come as a stranger, dear Miss
Beaufort,' writes generous Maria. 'You will not lead a
new life, but only continue to lead the life you have been
used to in your own happy cultivated family.' And her
stepmother in a few feeling words describes all that Maria
was to her from the very first when she came as a bride to
the home where the sisters and the children of the lately
lost wife were all assembled to meet her.

It gives an unpleasant thrill to read of the newly-
married lady coming along to her home in a postchaise, and
seeing something odd on the side of the road. 'Look to
the other side ; don't look at it,' says Mr. Edgeworth ; and
when they had passed he tells his bride that it was the
body of a man hung by the rebels between the shafts of a
car.

The family at Edgeworthtown consisted of two ladies, sisters of the late Mrs. Edgeworth, who made it their home, and of Maria, the last of the first family. Lovell, now the eldest son, was away ; but there were also four daughters and three sons at home.

All agreed in making me feel at once at home and part of the family ; all received me with the most unaffected cordiality ; but from Maria it was something more. She more than fulfilled the promise of her letter ; she made me at once her most intimate friend, and in every trifle of the day treated me with the most generous confidence.

Those times were even more serious than they are now ; we hear of Mr. Bond, the High Sheriff, paying ' a pale visit ' to Edgeworthtown. ' I am going on in the old way, writing stories,' says Maria Edgeworth, writing in 1798. ' I cannot be a captain of dragoons, and sitting with my hands before me would not make any one of us one degree safer. . . . Simple Susan went to Foxhall a few days ago for Lady Anne to carry her to England.' . . . ' My father has made our little rooms so nice for us,' she continues ; ' they are all fresh painted and papered. Oh ! rebels, oh ! French spare them. We have never injured you, and all we wish is to see everybody as happy as ourselves.'

On August 29 we find from Miss Edgeworth's letter to

H

her cousin that the French have got to Castlebar. 'The
Lord-Lieutenant is now at Athlone, and it is supposed it
will be their next object of attack. My father's corps of
yeomanry are extremely attached to him and seem fully in
earnest'; but, alas! by some strange negligence, their arms
have not yet arrived from Dublin. . . . We, who are so
near the scene of action, cannot by any means discover
what *number* of the French actually landed ; some say 800,
some 1,800, some 18,000.'

The family had a narrow escape that day, for two
officers, who were in charge of some ammunition, offered to
take them under their protection as far as Longford. Mr.
Edgeworth most fortunately detained them. 'Half an
hour afterwards, as we were quietly sitting in the portico,
we heard, as we thought close to us, the report of a pistol
or a clap of thunder which shook the house. The officer
soon after returned almost speechless ; he could hardly explain what had happened. The ammunition cart, containing nearly three barrels of gunpowder, took fire, and burnt
half-way on the road to Longford. The man who drove
the cart was blown to atoms. Nothing of him could be
found. Two of the horses were killed ; others were blown
to pieces, and their limbs scattered to a distance. The
head and body of a man were found a hundred and twenty
yards from the spot. . . . If we had gone with this

ammunition cart, we must have been killed. An hour or
two afterwards we were obliged to fly from Edgeworthtown. The pikemen, 300 in number, were within a mile
of the town; my mother and Charlotte and I rode; passed
the trunk of the dead man, bloody limbs of horses, and two
dead horses, by the help of men who pulled on our steeds
—all safely lodged now in Mrs. Fallon's inn.' 'Before we
had reached the place where the cart had been blown up,
says Mrs. Edgeworth, ' Mr. Edgeworth suddenly recollected
that he had left on the table in his study a list of the
yeomanry corps which he feared might endanger the poor
fellows and their families if it fell into the hands of the
rebels. He galloped back for it. It was at the hazard of
his life; but the rebels had not yet appeared. He burned
the paper, and rejoined us safely.' The Memoirs give a
most interesting and spirited account of the next few days.
The rebels spared Mr. Edgeworth's house, although they
broke into it. After a time the family were told that all
was safe for their return, and the account of their coming
home, as it is given in the second volume of Mr. Edgeworth's life by his daughter, is a model of style and
admirable description.

In 1799 Mr. Edgeworth came into Parliament for the
borough of St. Johnstown. He was a Unionist by conviction, but he did not think the times were yet ripe for

the Union, and he therefore voted against it. In some of his letters to Dr. Darwin written at this time, he says that he was offered 3,000 guineas for his seat for the few remaining weeks of the session, which, needless to say, he refused, not thinking it well, as he says, '*to quarrel with myself.*' He also adds that Maria continues writing for children under the persuasion that she cannot be more serviceably employed ; and he sends (with his usual perspicuity) affectionate messages to the Doctor's 'good amiable lady and *his giant brood.*' But this long friendly correspondence was coming to an end. The Doctor's letters, so quietly humorous and to the point, Mr. Edgeworth's answers with all their characteristic and lively variety, were nearly at an end.

It was in 1800 that Maria had achieved her great success, and published 'Castle Rackrent,' a book—not for children this time—which made everybody talk who read, and those read who had only talked before. This work was published anonymously, and so great was its reputation that some one was at the pains to copy out the whole of the story with erasures and different signs of authenticity, and assume the authorship.

One very distinctive mark of Maria Edgeworth's mind is the honest candour and genuine critical faculty which is hers. Her appreciation of her own work and that of others is unaffected and really discriminating, whether it is 'Corinne' or a simple story which she is reading, or Scott's new novel the 'Pirate,' or one of her own manuscripts which she estimates justly and reasonably. 'I have read "Corinne" with my father, and I like it better than he does. In one word, I am dazzled by the genius, provoked by the absurdities, and in admiration of the taste and critical judgment of Italian literature displayed throughout the whole work: but I will not dilate upon it in a letter. I could talk for three hours to you and my aunt.'

Elsewhere she speaks with the warmest admiration of a 'Simple Story.' Jane Austen's books were not yet published; but another writer, for whom Mr. Edgeworth and his daughter had a very great regard and admiration, was Mrs. Barbauld, who in all the heavy trials and sorrows of her later life found no little help and comfort in the friendship and constancy of Maria Edgeworth. Mr. and Mrs. Barbauld, upon Mr. Edgeworth's invitation, paid him a visit at Clifton, where he was again staying in 1799, and where the last Mrs. Edgeworth's eldest child was born. There is a little anecdote of domestic life at this time in the Memoirs which gives one a glimpse, not of an authoress, but of a very sympathising and impressionable person. 'Maria took her little sister to bring down to her father, but when she had descended a few steps a panic seized her, and she was afraid to go either backwards or forwards. She sat down on the stairs afraid she should drop the child, afraid that its head would come off, and afraid that her father would find her sitting there and laugh at her, till seeing the footman passing she called "Samuel" in a terrified voice, and made him walk before her backwards down the stairs till she safely reached the sitting-room.' For all these younger children Maria seems to have had a most tender and motherly regard, as indeed for all her young brothers and sisters of the different families. Many of them were the heroines of her various stories, and few heroines are more charming than some of Miss Edgeworth's. Rosamund is said by some to have been Maria herself, impulsive, warm-hearted, timid, and yet full of spirit and animation.

In his last letter to Mr. Edgeworth Dr. Darwin writes kindly of the authoress, and sends her a message. The letter is dated April 17, 1802. ' I am glad to find you still amuse yourself with mechanism in spite of the troubles of Ireland;' and the Doctor goes on to ask his friend to come and pay a visit to the Priory, and describes the pleasant house with the garden, the ponds full of fish, the deep umbrageous valley, with the talkative stream running down it, and Derby tower in the distance. The letter, so kind, so playful in its tone, was never finished. Dr. Darwin was writing as he was seized with what seemed a fainting fit, and he died within an hour. Miss Edgeworth writes of the shock her father felt when the sad news reached him; a shock, she says, which must in some degree be experienced by every person who reads this letter of Dr. Darwin's.

No wonder this generous outspoken man was esteemed in his own time. To us, in ours, it has been given still more to know the noble son of 'that giant brood,' whose name will be loved and held in honour as long as people live to honour nobleness, simplicity, and genius; those things which give life to life itself.

## VIII.

'Calais after a rough passage; Brussels, flat country, tiled houses, trees and ditches, the window shutters turned out to the street; fishwives' legs, Dunkirk, and the people looking like wooden toys set in motion; Bruges and its mingled spires, shipping, and windmills.' These notes of travel read as if Miss Edgeworth had been writing down only yesterday a pleasant list of the things which are to be seen two hours off, to-day no less plainly than a century ago. She jots it all down from her corner in the postchaise, where she is propped up with a father, brother, stepmother, and sister for travelling companions, and a new book to beguile the way. She is charmed with her new book. It is the story of 'Mademoiselle de Clermont,' by Madame de Genlis, and only just out. The Edgeworths (with many other English people) rejoiced in the long-looked-for millennium, which had been signed only the previous autumn, and they now came abroad to bask in the sunshine of the Continent, which had been so long denied to our mist-bound islanders. We hear of the enthusiastic and somewhat premature joy with which this peace was received by all ranks of people. Not only did the English rush over to France; foreigners crossed to England, and one of them, an old friend of Mr. Edgeworth's, had already reached Edgeworthtown, and inspired its enterprising master with a desire to see those places and things once more which he heard described. Mr. Edgeworth was anxious also to show his young wife the treasures in the Louvre, and to help her to develop her taste for art. He had had many troubles of late, lost friends and children by death and by marriage. One can imagine that the change must have been welcome to them all. Besides Maria and Lovell, his eldest son, he took with him a lovely young daughter, Charlotte Edgeworth, the daughter of Elizabeth Sneyd. They travelled by Belgium, stopping on their way at Bruges, at Ghent, and visiting pictures and churches along the road, as travellers still like to do. Mrs. Edgeworth was, as we have said, the artistic member of the party. We do not know what modern rhapsodists would say to Miss Edgeworth's very subdued criticisms and descriptions of feeling on this occasion. ' It is extremely agreeable to me,' she writes, ' to see paintings with those who have excellent taste and no affectation.' And this remark might perhaps be thought even more to the point now than in the pre-æsthetic age in which it was innocently made. The travellers are finally landed in Paris in a magnificent hotel in a fine square, 'formerly Place Louis-Quinze, afterwards Place de la Révolution, now Place de la Concorde.' And Place de la Concorde it remains, wars and revolutions notwithstanding, whether lighted by the flames of the desperate Commune or by the peaceful sunsets which stream their evening glory across the blood-stained stones.

The Edgeworths did not come as strangers to Paris ; they brought letters and introductions with them, and bygone associations and friendships which had only now to be resumed. The well-known Abbé Morellet, their old acquaintance, ' answered for them,' says Miss Edgeworth, and besides all this Mr Edgeworth's name was well known in scientific circles. Bréguet, Montgolfier, and others all made him welcome. Lord Henry Petty, as Maria's friend Lord Lansdowne was then called, was in Paris, and Rogers the poet, and Kosciusko, cured of his wounds. For the first time they now made the acquaintance of M. Dumont, a lifelong friend and correspondent. There were many others—the Delesserts, of the French Protestant faction, Madame Suard, to whom the romantic Thomas Day had paid court some thirty years before, and Madame Campan, and Madame Récamier, and Madame de Rémusat, and Madame de Houdetot, now seventy-two years of age, but Rousseau's Julie still, and Camille Jordan, and the Chevalier Edelcrantz, from the Court of the King of Sweden.

The names alone of the Edgeworths' entertainers represent a delightful and interesting section of the history of the time. One can imagine that besides all these pleasant and talkative persons the Faubourg Saint-Germain itself threw open its great swinging doors to the relations of the Abbé Edgeworth who risked his life to stand by his master upon the scaffold and to speak those noble warm-hearted words, the last that Louis ever heard. One can picture the family party as it must have appeared with its pleasant British looks—the agreeable 'ruddy-faced' father, the gentle Mrs. Edgeworth, who is somewhere described by her stepdaughter as so orderly, so clean, so

freshly dressed, the child of fifteen, only too beautiful
and delicately lovely, and last of all Maria herself, the
nice little unassuming, Jeannie-Deans-looking body Lord
Byron described, small, homely, perhaps, but with her
gift of French, of charming intercourse, her fresh laurels
of authorship (for ' Belinda ' was lately published), her
bright animation, her cultivated mind and power of interesting all those in her company, to say nothing of her own
kindling interest in every one and every thing round about
her.

Her keen delights and vivid descriptions of all these
new things, faces, voices, ideas, are all to be read in some
long and most charming letters to Ireland, which also
contain the account of a most eventful crisis which this
Paris journey brought about. The letter is dated March
1803, and it concludes as follows :—

Here, my dear aunt, I was interrupted in a manner that will
surprise you as much as it surprised me—by the coming of M.
Edelcrantz, a Swedish gentleman whom we have mentioned to
you, of superior understanding and mild manners. He came to
offer me his hand and heart ! My heart, you may suppose,
cannot return his attachment, for I have seen but very little of
him, and have not had time to have formed any judgment except
that I think nothing could tempt me to leave my own dear
friends and my own country to live in Sweden.

Maria Edgeworth was now about thirty years of age, at

a time of life when people are apt to realise perhaps almost more deeply than in early youth the influence of feeling, its importance, and strange power over events. Hitherto there are no records in her memoirs of any sentimental episodes, but it does not follow that a young lady has not had her own phase of experience because she does not write it out at length to her various aunts and correspondents. Miss Edgeworth was not a sentimental person. She was warmly devoted to her own family, and she seems to have had a strong idea of her own want of beauty ; perhaps her admiration for her lovely young sisters may have caused this feeling to be exaggerated by her. But no romantic, lovely heroine could have inspired a deeper or more touching admiration than this one which M. Edelcrantz felt for his English friend ; the mild and superior Swede seems to have been thoroughly in earnest.

So indeed was Miss Edgeworth, but she was not carried away by the natural impulse of the moment. She realised the many difficulties and dangers of the unknown ; she looked to the future ; she turned to her own home, and with an affection all the more felt because of the trial to which it was now exposed. The many lessons of self-control and self-restraint which she had learnt returned with instinctive force. Sometimes it happens that people miss what is perhaps the best for the sake of the next best, and we see convenience and old habit and expediency, and a hundred small and insignificant circumstances, gathering like some avalanche to divide hearts that might give and receive very much from each. But sentiment is not the only thing in life. Other duties, ties, and realities there are ; and it is difficult to judge for others in such matters. Sincerity of heart and truth to themselves are pretty sure in the end to lead people in the right direction for their own and for other people's happiness. Only, in the experience of many women there is the danger that fixed ideas, and other people's opinion, and the force of custom may limit lives which might have been complete in greater things, though perhaps less perfect in the lesser. People in the abstract are sincere enough in wishing fulness of experience and of happiness to those dearest and nearest to them ; but we are only human beings, and when the time comes and the horrible necessity for parting approaches, our courage goes, our hearts fail, and we think we are preaching reason and good sense while it is only a most natural instinct which leads us to cling to that to which we are used and to those we love.

Mr. Edgeworth did not attempt to influence Maria. Mrs. Edgeworth evidently had some misgivings, and certainly much sympathy for the Chevalier and for her friend and stepdaughter. She says :—

Maria was mistaken as to her own feelings. She refused M. Edelcrantz, but she felt much more for him than esteem and admiration ; she was extremely in love with him. Mr. Edgeworth left her to decide for herself; but she saw too plainly what it would be to us to lose her and what she would feel at parting with us. She decided rightly for her own future happiness and for that of her family, but she suffered much at the time and long afterwards. While we were at Paris I remember that in a shop, where Charlotte and I were making purchases, Maria sat apart absorbed in thought, and so deep in reverie that when her father came in and stood opposite to her she did not see him till he spoke to her, when she started and burst into tears. . . . I do not think she repented of her refusal or regretted her decision. She was well aware that she could not have made M. Edelcrantz happy, that she would not have suited his position at the Court of Stockholm, and that her want of beauty might have diminished his attachment. It was perhaps better she should think so, for it calmed her mind ; but from what I saw of M. Edelcrantz I think he was a man capable of really valuing her. I believe he was much attached to her, and deeply mortified at her refusal. He continued to reside in Sweden after the abdication of his master, and was always distinguished for his high character and great abilities. He never married. He was, except for his very fine eyes, remarkably plain.

So ends the romance of the romancer. There are, however, many happinesses in life, as there are many troubles.

Mrs. Edgeworth tells us that after her stepdaughter's return to Edgeworthtown she occupied herself with various literary works, correcting some of her former MSS. for the press, and writing 'Madame de Fleury,' 'Emilie de Coulanges,' and 'Leonora.' But the high-flown and romantic style did suit her gift, and she wrote best when her genuine interest and unaffected glances shone with bright understanding sympathy upon her immediate surroundings. When we are told that 'Leonora' was written in the style the Chevalier Edelcrantz preferred, and that the idea of what he would think of it was present to Maria in every page, we begin to realise that for us at all events it was a most fortunate thing that she decided as she did. It would have been a loss indeed to the world if this kindling and delightful spirit of hers had been choked by the polite thorns, fictions, and platitudes of an artificial, courtly life and by the well-ordered narrowness of a limited standard. She never heard what the Chevalier thought of the book; she never knew that he ever read it even. It is a satisfaction to hear that he married no one else, and while she sat writing and not forgetting in the pleasant library at home, one can imagine the romantic Chevalier in his distant Court faithful to the sudden and romantic devotion by which he is now remembered. Romantic and chivalrous friendship seems to belong to his country and to his countrymen.

## IX.

There are one or two other episodes less sentimental
than this one recorded of this visit to Paris, not the least
interesting of these being the account given of a call
upon Madame de Genlis.  The younger author from her
own standpoint having resolutely turned away from the voice
of the charmer for the sake of that which she is convinced
to be duty and good sense, now somewhat sternly takes the
measure of her elder sister, who has failed in the struggle,
who is alone and friendless, and who has made her fate.

The story is too long to quote at full length.  An
isolated page without its setting loses very much; the
previous description of the darkness and uncertainty
through which Maria and her father go wandering, and
asking their way in vain, adds immensely to the sense of
the gloom and isolation which are hiding the close of a
long and brilliant career.  At last, after wandering for a
long time seeking for Madame de Genlis, the travellers
compel a reluctant porter to show them the staircase in
the Arsenal, where she is living, and to point out the door
before he goes off with the light.

They wait in darkness.  The account of what happens
when the door is opened is so interesting that I cannot
refrain from quoting it at length :—

After ringing the bell we presently heard doors open and little footsteps approaching nigh. The door was opened by a girl of about Honora's size, holding an ill set-up, wavering candle in her hand, the light of which fell full upon her face and figure. Her face was remarkably intelligent—dark spark-ling eyes, dark hair curled in the most fashionable long cork-screw ringlets over her eyes and cheeks. She parted the ringlets to take a full view of us. The dress of her figure by no means suited the head and elegance of her attitude. What her nether weeds might be we could not distinctly see, but they seemed a coarse short petticoat like what Molly Bristow's children would wear. After surveying us and hearing our name was Edgeworth she smiled graciously and bid us follow her, saying, 'Maman est chez elle.' She led the way with the grace of a young lady who has been taught to dance across two ante-chambers, miserable-looking ; but, miserable or not, no home in Paris can be without them. The girl, or young lady, for we were still in doubt which to think her, led into a small room in which the candles were so well screened by a green tin screen that we could scarcely distinguish the tall form of a lady in black who rose from her chair by the fireside ; as the door opened a great puff of smoke came from the huge fireplace at the same moment. She came forward, and we made our way towards her as well as we could through a confusion of tables, chairs, and work-baskets, china, writing-desks and inkstands, and birdcages, and a harp. She did not speak, and as her back was now turned to both fire and candle I could not see her face or anything but the outline of her form and her attitude. Her form was the remains of a fine form, her attitude that of a woman used to a better drawing-room.

I being foremost, and she silent, was compelled to speak to the figure in darkness. 'Madame de Genlis nous a fait l'honneur de nous mander qu'elle voulait bien nous permettre de lui rendre

I

visite,' said I, or words to that effect, to which she replied by taking my hand and saying something in which ' charmée ' was the most intelligible word. While she spoke she looked over my shoulder at my father, whose bow, I presume, told her he was a gentleman, for she spoke to him immediately as if she wished to please and seated us in *fauteuils* near the fire.

I then had a full view of her face—figure very thin and melancholy dark eyes, long sallow cheeks, compressed thin lips, two or three black ringlets on a high forehead, a cap that Mrs. Grier might wear—altogether in appearance of fallen fortunes, worn-out health, and excessive but guarded irritability. To me there was nothing of that engaging, captivating manner which I had been taught to expect. She seemed to me to be alive only to literary quarrels and jealousies. The muscles of her face as she spoke, or as my father spoke to her, quickly and too easily expressed hatred and anger. . . . She is now, you know, *dévote acharnée.* . . . Madame de Genlis seems to have been so much used to being attacked that she has defence and apologies ready prepared. She spoke of Madame de Staël's ' Delphine ' with detestation. . . . Forgive me, my dear Aunt Mary ; you begged me to see her with favourable eyes, and I went, after seeing her ' Rosière de Salency,' with the most favourable disposition, but I could not like her. . . . And from time to time I saw, or thought I saw, through the gloom of her countenance a gleam of coquetry. But my father judges of her much more favourably than I do. She evidently took pains to please him, and he says he is sure she is a person over whose mind he could gain great ascendency.

The ' young and gay philosopher ' at fifty is not unchanged since we knew him first. Maria adds a post-script : –

I had almost forgotten to tell you that the little girl who showed us in is a girl whom she is educating. ' Elle m'appelle maman, mais elle n'est pas ma fille.' The manner in which this little girl spoke to Madame de Genlis and looked at her appeared to me more in her favour than anything else. I went to look at what the child was writing ; she was translating Darwin's *Zoonomia.*

Every description one reads by Miss Edgeworth of actual things and people makes one wish that she had written more of them. This one is the more interesting from the contrast of the two women, both so remarkable and coming to so different a result in their experience of life.

This eventful visit to Paris is brought to an eventful termination by several gendarmes, who appear early one morning in Mr. Edgeworth's bedroom with orders that he is to get up and to leave Paris immediately. Mr. Edgeworth had been accused of being brother to the Abbé de Fermont. When the mitigated circumstances of his being only a first cousin were put forward by Lord Whitworth, the English Ambassador, the Edgeworths received permission to return from the suburb to which they had retired ; but private news hurried their departure, and they were only in time to escape the general blockade and detention of English prisoners. After little more than a year of peace, once more war was declared on May 20, 1803.

Lovell, the eldest son, who was absent at the time and travelling from Switzerland, was not able to escape in time; nor for twelve years to come was the young man able to return to his own home and family.

## X.

'Belinda,' 'Castle Rackrent,' the 'Parents' Assistant,' the 'Essays on Practical Education,' had all made their mark. The new series of popular tales was also welcomed. There were other books on the way; Miss Edgeworth had several MSS. in hand in various stages, stories to correct for the press. There was also a long novel, first begun by her father and taken up and carried on by her. The 'Essays on Practical Education,' which were first published in 1798, continued to be read. M. Pictet had translated the book into French the year before; a third edition was published some ten years later, in 1811, in the preface of which the authors say, 'It is due to the public to state that twelve years' additional experience in a numerous family, and careful attention to the results of other modes of education, have given the authors no reason to retract what they have advanced in these volumes.'

In Mr. Edgeworth's Memoirs, however, his daughter states that he modified his opinions in one or two particulars; allowing more and more liberty to the children, and at the same time conceding greater importance to the habit of early though mechanical efforts of memory. The essays seem in every way in advance of their time; many of the hints contained in them most certainly apply to the little children of to-day no less than to their small grandparents. A lady whose own name is high in the annals of education was telling me that she had been greatly struck by the resemblance between the Edgeworth system and that of Froebel's Kindergarten method, which is now gaining more and more ground in people's estimation, the object of both being not so much to cram instruction into early youth as to draw out each child's powers of observation and attention.

The first series of tales of fashionable life came out in 1809, and contained among other stories 'Ennui,' one of the most remarkable of Miss Edgeworth's works. The second series included the 'Absentee,' that delightful story of which the lesson should be impressed upon us even more than in the year 1812. The 'Absentee' was at first only an episode in the longer novel of 'Patronage;' but the public was impatient, so were the publishers, and fortunately for every one the 'Absentee' was printed as a separate tale.

'Patronage' had been begun by Mr. Edgeworth to amuse his wife, who was recovering from illness; it was originally called the 'Fortunes of the Freeman Family, and it is a history with a moral. Morals were more in fashion then than they are now, but this one is obvious without any commentary upon it. It is tolerably certain that clever, industrious, well-conducted people will succeed, where idle, scheming, and untrustworthy persons will eventually fail to get on, even with powerful friends to back them. But the novel has yet to be written that will prove that, where merits are more equal, a little patronage is not of a great deal of use, or that people's positions in life are exactly proportioned to their merit. Mrs. Barbauld's pretty essay on the 'Inconsistency of Human Expectations' contains the best possible answer to the problem of what people's deserts should be. Let us hope that personal advancement is only one of the many things people try for in life, and that there are other prizes as well worth having. Miss Edgeworth herself somewhere speaks with warm admiration of this very essay. Of the novel itself she says (writing to Mrs. Barbauld), 'It is so vast a subject that it flounders about in my hands and quite overpowers me.'

It is in this same letter that Miss Edgeworth mentions another circumstance which interested her at this time, and which was one of those events occurring now and again which do equal credit to all concerned.

I have written a preface and notes [she says]—for I too would be an editor—fcr a little book which a very worthy countrywoman of mine is going to publish : Mrs. Leadbeater, granddaughter to Burke's first preceptor. She is poor. She has behaved most handsomely about some letters of Burke's to her grandfather and herself. It would have been advantageous to her to publish them ; but, as Mrs. Burke[1]—Heaven knows why—objected, she desisted.

Mrs. Leadbeater was an Irish Quaker lady whose simple and spirited annals of Ballitore delighted Carlyle in his later days, and whose 'Cottage Dialogues' greatly struck Mr. Edgeworth at the time ; and the kind Edgeworths, finding her quite unused to public transactions, exerted themselves in every way to help her. Mr. Edgeworth took the MSS. out of the hands of an Irish publisher, and, says Maria, 'our excellent friend's worthy successor in St. Paul's Churchyard has, on our recommendation, agreed to publish it for her.' Mr. Edgeworth's own letter to Mrs. Leadbeater gives the history of his good-natured offices and their satisfactory results.

---

[1] Mrs. Burke, hearing more of the circumstances, afterwards sent permission; but Mrs. Leadbeater being a Quakeress, and having once *promised* not to publish, could not take it upon herself to break her covenant.

From R. L. Edgeworth, July 5, 1810.

Miss Edgeworth desires me as a man of business to write
to Mrs. Leadbeater relative to the publication of 'Cottage
Dialogues.' Miss Edgeworth has written an advertisement, and
will, with Mrs. Leadbeater's permission, write notes for an
English edition.   The scheme which I propose is of two parts
—to sell the English copyright to the house of Johnson in
London, where we dispose of our own works, and to publish a
very large and cheap edition for Ireland for schools. . . . I can
probably introduce the book into many places.   Our family
takes 300 copies, Lady Longford 50, Dr. Beaufort 20, &c. . . .
I think Johnson & Co. will give 50*l.* for the English copyright.

After the transaction Mr. Edgeworth wrote to the
publishers as follows :—

> May 31, 1811 : Edgeworthtown.
> My sixty-eighth birthday.

My dear Gentlemen,—I have just heard your letter to
Mrs. Leadbeater read by one who dropped tears of pleasure
from a sense of your generous and handsome conduct.   I take
great pleasure in speaking of you to the rest of the world as
you deserve, and I cannot refrain from expressing to yourselves
the genuine esteem that I feel for you.   I know that this direct
praise is scarcely allowable, but my advanced age and my close
connection with you must be my excuse.—Yours sincerely,

> R. L. E.

Tears seem equivalent to something more than the
estimated value of Mrs. Leadbeater's labours.   The
charming and well-known Mrs. Trench who was also Mary
Leadbeater's friend, writes warmly praising the notes.
' Miss Edgeworth's notes on your Dialogues have as much

spirit and originality as if she had never before explored the mine which many thought she had exhausted.'

All these are pleasant specimens of the Edgeworth correspondence, which, however (following the course of most correspondence), does not seem to have been always equally agreeable. There are some letters (among others which I have been allowed to see) written by Maria about this time to an unfortunate young man who seems to have annoyed her greatly by his excited importunities.

I thank you [she says] for your friendly zeal in defence of my powers of pathos and sublimity; but I think it carries you much too far when it leads you to imagine that I refrain, from principle or virtue, from displaying powers that I really do not possess. I assure you that I am not in the least capable of writing a dithyrambic ode, or any other kind of ode.

One is reminded by this suggestion of Jane Austen also declining to write ' an historical novel illustrative of the august House of Coburg.'

The young man himself seems to have had some wild aspirations after authorship, but to have feared criticism.

The advantage of the art of printing [says his friendly Minerva] is that the mistakes of individuals in reasoning and writing will be corrected in time by the public, so that the cause of truth cannot suffer; and I presume you are too much of a philosopher to mind the trifling mortification that the detection of a mistake might occasion. You know that some sensible person has observed that acknowledging a mistake is

saying, only in other words, that we are wiser to-day than we
were yesterday.

He seems at last to have passed the bounds of reasonable correspondence, and she writes as follows :—

Your last letter, dated in June, was many months before it
reached me. In answer to all your reproaches at my silence I
can only assure you that it was not caused by any change in
my opinions or good wishes ; but I do not carry on what`is
called a regular correspondence with anybody except with one
or two of my very nearest relations; and it is best to tell the
plain truth that my father particularly dislikes my writing
letters, so I write as few as I possibly can.

## XI.

While Maria Edgeworth was at work in her Irish
home, successfully producing her admirable delineations,
another woman, born some eight years later, and living in
the quiet Hampshire village where the elm trees spread so
greenly, was also at work, also writing books that were
destined to influence many a generation, but which were
meanwhile waiting unknown, unnoticed. Do we not all
know the story of the brown paper parcel lying unopened
for years on the publisher's shelf and containing Henry
Tilney and all his capes, Catherine Morland and all her
romance, and the great John Thorpe himself, uttering those
valuable literary criticisms which Lord Macaulay, writing
to his little sisters at home, used to quote to them ?  ' Oh,

Lord!' says John Thorpe, 'I never read novels; I have other things to do.'

A friend reminds us of Miss Austen's own indignant outburst. ' Only a novel! only " Cecilia," or " Camilla," or " Belinda ; " or, in short, only some work in which the greatest powers of the mind are displayed, the most thorough knowledge of human nature, the happiest delineation of its varieties, the liveliest effusions of wit and humour, are conveyed to the world in the best-chosen language.' If the great historian, who loved novels himself, had not assured us that we owe Miss Austen and Miss Edgeworth to the early influence of the author of ' Evelina,' one might grudge ' Belinda ' to such company as that of ' Cecilia ' and ' Camilla.'

' Pride and Prejudice ' and ' Northanger Abbey ' were published about the same time as ' Patronage ' and ' Tales of Fashionable Life.' Their two authors illustrate, curiously enough, the difference between the national characteristics of English and Irish—the breadth, the versatility, the innate wit and gaiety of an Irish mind ; the comparative narrowness of range of an English nature ; where, however, we are more likely to get humour and its never-failing charm. Long afterwards Jane Austen sent one of her novels to Miss Edgeworth, who appreciated it indeed, as such a mind as hers could not fail to do, but it was with no such enthusiasm as that which she felt for other more ambitious works, with more of incident, power, knowledge of the world, in the place of that one subtle quality of humour which for some persons outweighs almost every other. Something, some indefinite sentiment, tells people where they amalgamate and with whom they are intellectually akin ; and by some such process of criticism the writer feels that in this little memoir of Miss Edgeworth she has but sketched the outer likeness of this remarkable woman's life and genius ; and that she has scarcely done justice to very much in Miss Edgeworth, which so many of the foremost men of her day could appreciate—a power, a versatility, an interest in subjects for their own sakes, not for the sakes of those who are interested in them, which was essentially hers.

It is always characteristic to watch a writer's progress in the estimation of critics and reviewers. In 1809 Miss Edgeworth is moderately and respectfully noticed. ' As a writer of novels and tales she has a marked peculiarity, that of venturing to dispense common sense to her readers and to bring them within the precincts of real life. Without excluding love from her pages she knows how to assign to it its true limits.' In 1812 the reviewer, more used to hear the author's praises on all sides, now starts from a higher key, and, as far as truth to nature and delineation

of character are concerned, does not allow a rival except
' Don Quixote ' and ' Gil Blas.' The following criticism
is just and more to the point :—

> To this power of masterly and minute delineation of cha-
> racter Miss Edgeworth adds another which has rarely been
> combined with the former, that of interweaving the peculiarities
> of her persons with the conduct of her piece, and making them,
> without forgetting for a moment their personal consistency,
> conduce to the general lesson. . . . Her virtue and vice,
> though copied exactly from nature, lead with perfect ease to a
> moral conclusion, and are finally punished or rewarded by
> means which (rare as a retribution in this world is) appear for
> the most part neither inconsistent nor unnatural.

Then follows a review of ' Vivian ' and of the ' Absentee,'
which is perhaps the most admirable of her works. We
may all remember how Macaulay once pronounced that
the scene in the ' Absentee ' where Lord Colambre dis-
covers himself to his tenantry was the best thing of the
sort since the opening of the twenty-second book of the
' Odyssey.'

An article by Lord Dudley, which is still to be quoted,
appeared in the ' Quarterly Review ' in 1814. What he
says of her works applies no less to Miss Edgeworth's own
life than to the principles which she inculcates.

> The old rule was for heroes and heroines to fall suddenly
> and irretrievably in love. If they fell in love with the right
> person so much the better ; if not, it could not be helped, and

the novel ended unhappily. And, above all, it was held quite irregular for the most reasonable people to make any use whatever of their reason on the most important occasion of their lives. Miss Edgeworth has presumed to treat this mighty power with far less reverence. She has analysed it and found it does not consist of one simple element, but that several common ingredients enter into its composition—habit, esteem, a belief of some corresponding sentiment and of suitableness in the character and circumstances of the party. She has pronounced that reason, timely and vigorously applied, is almost a specific, and, following up this bold empirical line of practice, she has actually produced cases of the entire cure of persons who had laboured under its operation. Her favourite qualities are prudence, firmness, temper, and that active, vigilant good sense which, without checking the course of our kind affections, exercises its influence at every moment and surveys deliberately the motives and consequences of every action. Utility is her object, reason and experience her means.

## XII.

This review of Lord Dudley's must have come out after a visit from the Edgeworth family to London in 1813, which seems to have been a most brilliant and amusing campaign. ' I know the homage that was paid you,' wrote Mrs. Barbauld, speaking of the event, 'and I exulted in it for your sake and for my sex's sake.' Miss Edgeworth was at the height of her popularity, in good spirits and good health. Mr. Edgeworth was seventy, but he looked years younger, and was still in undiminished health and vigour. The party was welcomed, fêted, sought after everywhere. Except that they miss seeing Madame d'Arblay and leave London before the arrival of Madame de Staël, they seem to have come in for everything that was brilliant, fashionable, and entertaining. They breakfast with poets, they sup with marquises, they call upon duchesses and scientific men. Maria's old friend the Duchess of Wellington is not less her friend than she was in County Longford. Every one likes them and comes knocking at their lodging-house door, while Maria upstairs is writing a letter. standing at a chest of drawers. 'Miss Edgeworth is delightful,' says Tom Moore, 'not from display, but from repose and unaffectedness, the least pretending person.' Even Lord Bryon writes warmly of the authoress whose company is so grateful, and who goes her simple, pleasant way cheerful and bringing kind cheer, and making friends with the children as well as with the elders. Many of these children in their lives fully justified her interest, children whom we in turn have known and looked up to as distinguished greyheaded men.

Some one asked Miss Edgeworth how she came to understand children as she did, what charm she used to win them. 'I don't know,' she said kindly; 'I lie down and let them crawl over me.' She was greatly pleased on one occasion when at a crowded party a little girl suddenly

started forth, looked at her hard, and said, ' I like simple
Susan best,' and rushed away overwhelmed at her own
audacity. The same lady who was present on this occasion
asked her a question which we must all be grateful to have
solved for us—how it happened that the respective places
of Laura and Rosamond came to be transposed in
' Patronage,' Laura having been the wiser elder sister in
the ' Purple Jar,' and appearing suddenly as the younger
in the novel. Miss Edgeworth laughed and said that
Laura had been so preternaturally wise and thoughtful as
a child, she could never have kept her up to the mark, and
so she thought it best to change the character altogether.

During one of her visits to London Miss Edgeworth
went to dine at the house of Mr. Marshall ; and his
daughter, Lady Monteagle, tells a little story which gives
an impression, and a kind one, of the celebrated guest.
Everything had been prepared in her honour, the lights
lighted, the viands were cooked. Dinner was announced,
and some important person was brought forward to hand
Miss Edgeworth down, when it was discovered that she
had vanished. For a moment the company and the dinner
were all at a standstill. She was a small person, but
diligent search was made. Miss Edgeworth had last been
seen with the children of the house, and she was eventually
found in the back kitchen, escorted by the said children,

who, having confided their private affairs to her sympathetic ear, had finally invited her to come with them
and see some rabbits which they were rearing down below.
A lady who used to live at Clifton as a little girl, and to
be sometimes prescribed for by Dr. King, was once brought
up as a child to Miss Edgeworth, and she told me how very
much puzzled she felt when the bright old lady, taking her
by the hand, said, ' Well, my dear, how do you do, and how
is my excellent brother-in-law ?' One can imagine what a
vague sort of being an 'excellent brother-in-law' would
seem to a very young child.

We read in Miss Edgeworth's memoir of her father
that Mr. Edgeworth recovered from his serious illness in
1814 to enjoy a few more years of life among his friends,
his children, and his experiments. His good humour and
good spirits were undiminished, and he used to quote an
old friend's praise of 'the privileges and convenience of
old age.' He was past seventy, but he seems to have
continued his own education to the end of life. ' Without
affecting to be young, he exerted himself to prevent any of
his faculties from sinking into the indolent state which
portends their decay,' and his daughter says that he went
on learning to the last, correcting his faults and practising
his memory by various devices, so that it even improved
with age.

K

In one of his last letters to Mrs. Beaufort, his wife's mother, he speaks with no little paternal pleasure of his home and his children : ' Such excellent principles, such just views of human life and manners, such cultivated understandings, such charming tempers make a little Paradise about me ; ' while with regard to his daughter's works he adds concerning the book which was about to appear, ' If Maria's tales fail with the public, you will hear of my hanging myself.'

Mr. Edgeworth died in the summer of 1817, at home, surrounded by his family, grateful, as he says, to Providence for allowing his body to perish before his mind.

During the melancholy months which succeeded her father's death Maria hardly wrote any letters ; her sight was in a most alarming state. The tears, she said, felt in her eyes like the cutting of a knife. She had overworked them all the previous winter, sitting up at night and struggling with her grief as she wrote ' Ormond.' She was now unable to use them without pain. . . . Edgeworthtown now belonged to Lovell, the eldest surviving brother, but he wished it to continue the home of the family. Maria set to work to complete her father's memoirs and to fulfil his last wish.

It was not without great hesitation and anxiety that she determined to finish writing her father's Life. There is a touching appeal in a letter to her aunt Ruxton. ' I felt the happiness of my life was at stake. Even if all the rest of the world had praised it and you had been dissatisfied, how miserable should I have been!' And there is another sentence written at Bowood, very sad and full of remembrance : 'I feel as if I had lived a hundred years and was left alive after everybody else.' The book came out, and many things were said about it, not all praise. The 'Quarterly' was so spiteful and intolerant that it seemed almost personal in its violence. It certainly would have been a great loss to the world had this curious and interesting memoir never been published, but at the time the absence of certain phrases and expressions of opinions which Mr. Edgeworth had never specially professed seemed greatly to offend the reviewers.

The worst of these attacks Miss Edgeworth never read, and the task finished, the sad months over, the poor eyes recovered, she crossed to England.


## XIII.

One is glad to hear of her away and at Bowood reviving in good company, in all senses of the word. Her old friend Lord Henry Petty, now Lord Lansdowne, was still her friend and full of kindness. Outside the house spread a green deer-park to rest her tired eyes, within were pleasant and delightful companions to cheer her soul. Sir Samuel

Romilly was there, of whom she speaks with affectionate admiration, as she does of her kind host and hostess. ' I much enjoy the sight of Lady Lansdowne's happiness with her husband and her children. Beauty, fortune, cultivated society all united—in short, everything that the most reasonable or unreasonable could wish. She is so amiable and desirous to make others happy.'

Miss Edgeworth's power of making other people see things as she does is very remarkable in all these letters; with a little imagination one could almost feel as if one might be able to travel back into the pleasant society in which she lived. When she goes abroad soon after with her two younger sisters (Fanny, the baby whose head so nearly came off in her arms, and Harriet, who have both grown up by this time to be pretty and elegant young ladies), the sisters are made welcome everywhere. In Paris, as in London, troops of acquaintance came forward to receive ' Madame Maria et mesdemoiselles ses sœurs,' as they used to be announced. Most of their old friends were there still; only the children had grown up and were now new friends to be greeted. It is a confusion of names in visionary succession, comprising English people no less than French. Miss Edgeworth notes it all with a sure hand and true pen; it is as one of the sketch-books of a great painter, where whole pictures are indicated in a few just lines. Here is a peep at the Abbaye aux Bois in 1820 :—

We went to Madame Récamier in her convent, l'Abbaye aux Bois, up seventy-eight steps. All came in with asthma. Elegant room; she as elegant as ever. Matthieu de Montmorenci, the ex-Queen of Sweden, Madame de Boigne, a charming woman, and Madame la Maréchale de ——, a battered beauty, smelling of garlic and screeching in vain to pass as a wit. . . . Madame Récamier has no more taken the veil than I have, and is as little likely to do it. She is quite beautiful ; she dresses herself and her little room with elegant simplicity, and lives in a convent only because it is cheap and respectable.

One sees it all, the convent, the company, the last refrain of former triumphs, the faithful romantic Matthieu de Montmorenci, and above all the poor Maréchale, who will screech for ever in her garlic. Let us turn the page, we find another picture from these not long past days :—

Breakfast at Camille Jordan's ; it was half-past twelve before the company assembled, and we had an hour's delightful conversation with Camille Jordan and his wife in her spotless white muslin and little cap, sitting at her husband's feet as he lay on the sofa ; as clean, as nice, as fresh, as thoughtless of herself as my mother. At this breakfast we saw three of the most distinguished of that party who call themselves ' les Doctrinaires ' and say they are more attached to measures than to men.

Here is another portrait of a portrait and its painter :—

Princess Potemkin is a Russian, but she has all the grace,

softness, winning manner of the Polish ladies.   Oval face, pale,
with the finest, softest, most expressive chestnut dark eyes.
She has a sort of politeness which pleases peculiarly, a mixture
of the ease of high rank and early habit with something that is
sentimental without affectation.   Madame le Brun is painting
her picture.   Madame le Brun is sixty-six, with great vivacity
as well as genius, and better worth seeing than her pictures,
for though they are speaking she speaks.

Another visit the sisters paid, which will interest the
readers of Madame de la Rochejaquelin's memoirs of the
war in the Vendée :—

In a small bedroom, well furnished, with a fire just lighted,
we found Madame de la Rochejaquelin on the sofa ; her two
daughters at work, one spinning with a distaff, the other
embroidering muslin.   Madame is a fat woman with a broad,
round, fair face and a most benevolent expression, her hair cut
short and perfectly grey as seen under her cap ; the rest of the
face much too young for such grey locks ; and though her face
and bundled form all squashed on to a sofa did not at first
promise much of gentility, you could not hear her speak or
hear her for three minutes without perceiving that she was
well-born and well-bred.

Madame de la Rochejaquelin seems to have confided in
Miss Edgeworth.

' I am always sorry when any stranger sees me, *parce que
je sais que je détruis toute illusion.   Je sais que je devrais
avoir l'air d'une héroïne.'*   She is much better than a heroine ;
she is benevolence and truth itself.

We must not forget the scientific world where Madame

Maria was no less at home than in fashionable literary cliques. The sisters saw something of Cuvier at Paris; in Switzerland they travelled with the Aragos. They were on their way to the Marcets at Geneva when they stopped at Coppet, where Miss Edgeworth was always specially happy in the society of Madame Auguste de Staël and Madame de Broglie. But Switzerland is not one of the places where human beings only are in the ascendant; other influences there are almost stronger than human ones. ' I did not conceive it possible that I should feel so much pleasure from the beauties of nature as I have done since I came to this country. The first moment when I saw Mont Blanc will remain an era in my life—a new idea, a new feeling standing alone in the mind.' Miss Edgeworth presently comes down from her mountain heights and, full of interest, throws herself into the talk of her friends at Coppet and Geneva, from which she quotes as it occurs to her. Here is Rocca's indignant speech to Lord Byron, who was abusing the stupidity of the Genevese. ' Eh ! milord, pourquoi venir vous fourrer parmi ces honnêtes gens ? ' There is Arago's curious anecdote of Napoleon, who sent for him after the battle of Waterloo, offering him a large sum of money to accompany him to America. The Emperor had formed a project for founding a scientific colony in the New World. Arago was so indignant with

him for abandoning his troops that he would have nothing
to say to the plan. A far more touching story is Dr.
Marcet's account of Josephine. 'Poor Josephine! Do you
remember Dr. Marcet's telling us that when he breakfasted
with her she said, pointing to her flowers, "These are my
subjects. I try to make them happy "?'

Among other expeditions they made a pilgrimage to the
home of the author of a work for which Miss Edgeworth
seems to have entertained a mysterious enthusiasm. The
novel was called 'Caroline de Lichfield,' and was so much
admired at the time that Miss Seward mentions a gentleman who wrote from abroad to propose for the hand of the
authoress, and who, more fortunate than the poor Chevalier
Edelcrantz, was not refused by the lady. Perhaps some
similarity of experience may have led Maria Edgeworth to
wish for her acquaintance. Happily the time was past for
Miss Edgeworth to look back ; her life was now shaped and
moulded in its own groove ; the consideration, the variety,
the difficulties of unmarried life were hers, its agreeable
change, its monotony of feeling and of unselfish happiness,
compared with the necessary regularity, the more personal
felicity, the less liberal interests of the married. Her life
seems to have been full to overflowing of practical occupation and consideration for others. What changing scenes
and colours, what a number of voices, what a crowd of out-

stretched hands, what interesting processions of people pass across her path! There is something of her father's optimism and simplicity of nature in her unceasing brightness and activity, in her resolutions to improve as time goes on. Her young brothers and sisters grow to be men and women ; with her sisters' marriages new interests touch her warm heart. Between her and the brothers of the younger generation who did not turn to her as a sort of mother there may have been too great a difference of age for that companionship to continue which often exists between a child and a grown-up person. So at least one is led to believe was the case as regards one of them, mentioned in a memoir which has recently appeared. But to her sisters she could be friend, protector, chaperon, sympathising companion, and elder sister to the end of her days. We hear of them all at Bowood again on their way back to Ireland, and then we find them all at home settling down to the old life, 'Maria reading Sévigné,' of whom she never tires.

## XIV.

One of the prettiest and most sympathetic incidents in Maria Edgeworth's life was a subsequent expedition to Abbotsford and the pleasure she gave to its master. They

first met in Edinburgh, and her short account conjures up
the whole scene before us :—

> Ten o'clock struck as I read this note.   We were tired, we
> were not fit to be seen, but I thought it right to accept Walter
> Scott's cordial invitation, sent for a hackney coach, and just as
> we were, without dressing, we went.   As the coach stopped we
> saw the hall lighted, and the moment the door opened heard the
> joyous sounds of loud singing.     Three servants' ' The Miss
> Edgeworths ! ' sounded from hall to landing-place, and as I
> paused for a moment in the anteroom 'I heard the first sound of
> Walter  Scott's  voice—' The  Miss  Edgeworths *come* ! '   The
> room was lighted by only one globe lamp ; a circle were singing
> loud and beating time : all stopped in an instant.

Is not this picture complete ?   Scott himself she
describes as ' full of genius without the slightest effort at
expression, delightfully natural, more lame but not so
unwieldy as she expected.'   Lady Scott she goes on to
sketch in some half-dozen words—' French, large dark
eyes, civil and good-natured.'

> When we wakened the next morning the whole scene of the
> preceding night seemed like a dream [she continues] ; however
> at twelve came the real Lady Scott, and we called for Scott at
> the Parliament House, who came out of the Courts with joyous
> face, as if he had nothing on earth to do or to think of but to
> show us Edinburgh.

In her quick, discriminating way she looks round and
notes them all one by one.

Mr. Lockhart is reserved and silent, but he appears to have much sensibility under this reserve. Mrs. Lockhart is very pleasing—a slight, elegant figure and graceful simplicity of manner, perfectly natural. There is something most winning in her affectionate manner to her father. He dotes upon her.

A serious illness intervened for poor Maria before she and her devoted young nurses could reach Abbotsford itself. There she began to recover, and Lady Scott watched over her and prescribed for her with the most tender care and kindness. ' Lady Scott felt the attention and respect Maria showed to her, perceiving that she valued her and treated her as a friend,' says Mrs. Edgeworth; ' not, as too many of Sir Walter's guests did, with neglect.' This is Miss Edgeworth's description of the Abbotsford family life :—

It is quite delightful to see Scott and his family in the country ; breakfast, dinner, supper, the same flow of kindness, fondness, and genius, far, far surpassing his works, his letters, and all my hopes and imagination. His Castle of Abbotsford is magnificent, but I forget it in thinking of him.

The return visit, when Scotland visited Ireland, was no less successful. Mrs. Edgeworth writes :—

Maria and my daughter Harriet accompanied Sir Walter and Miss Scott, Mr. Lockhart, and Captain and Mrs. Scott to Killarney. They travelled in an open calèche of Sir Walter's. . . .

Sir Walter was, like Maria, never put out by discomforts on
a journey, but always ready to make the best of everything and
to find amusement in every incident. He was delighted with
Maria's eagerness for everybody's comfort, and diverted himself
with her admiration of a green baize-covered door at the inn at
Killarney. 'Miss Edgeworth, you are so mightily pleased with
that door, I think you will carry it away with you to Edgeworthtown.'

Miss Edgeworth's friendships were certainly very remarkable, and comprise almost all the interesting people
of her day in France as well as in England.[1]　She was

---

[1] A touching illustration of her abiding influence is to be found cited
in an article in the *Daily News* of September 7, 1883, published as these
proofs are going to press, by 'One Who Knew' Ivan Turguéneff, that
great Russian whom we might almost claim if love and admiration gave
one a right to count citizenship with the great men of our time. An
elder brother of his knew Miss Edgeworth, perhaps at Abbotsford, for
he visited Walter Scott there, or at Coppet with Madame de Staël.
This man, wise and cultivated in all European literature, 'came to the
conclusion that Maria Edgeworth had struck on a vein from which
most of the great novelists of the future would exclusively work. She
took the world as she found it, and selected from it the materials that
she thought would be interesting to write about, in a clear and natural
style. It was Ivan Turguéneff himself who told me this, says the writer of
the article, and he modestly said that he was an unconscious disciple of
Miss Edgeworth in setting out on his literary career. He had not the
advantage of knowing English; but as a youth he used to hear his
brother translate to visitors at his country house in the Uralian Hills
passages from *Irish Tales and Sketches*, which he thought superior to
her three-volume novels. Turguéneff also said to me, " It is possible, nay
probable, that if Maria Edgeworth had not written about the poor Irish
of the co. Longford and the squires and squirees, that it would not have
occurred to me to give a literary form to my impressions about the classes
parallel to them in Russia. My brother used, in pointing out the
beauties of her unambitious works, to call attention to their extreme
simplicity and to the distinction with which she treated the simple
ones of the earth." '

liked, trusted, surrounded, and she appears to have had
the art of winning to her all the great men. We know
the Duke of Wellington addressed verses to her ; there
are pleasant intimations of her acquaintance with Sir
James Mackintosh, Romilly, Moore, and Rogers, and that
most delightful of human beings, Sydney Smith, whom
she thoroughly appreciated and admired. Describing her
brother Frank, she says, somewhere, ' I am much inclined
to think that he has a natural genius for happiness ; in
other words, as Sydney Smith would say, *great hereditary
constitutional joy.*' 'To attempt to Boswell Sydney
Smith's conversation would be to outboswell Boswell,' she
writes in another letter home ; but in Lady Holland's
memoir of her father there is a pleasant little account of
Miss Edgeworth herself, ' delightful, clever, and sensible,'
listening to Sydney Smith. She seems to have gone the
round of his parish with him while he scolded, doctored,
joked his poor people according to their needs.

' During her visit she saw much of my father,' says
Lady Holland ; ' and her talents as well as her thorough
knowledge and love of Ireland made her conversation
peculiarly agreeable to him.' On her side Maria writes
warmly desiring that some Irish bishopric might be forced
upon Sydney Smith, which ' his own sense of natural
charity and humanity would forbid him refuse . . . . In

the twinkling of an eye—such an eye as his—he would
see all our manifold grievances up and down the country.
One word, one *bon mot* of his, would do more for us, I
guess, than ——'s four hundred pages and all the like
with which we have been bored.'

The two knew how to make good company for one
another; the quiet-Jeanie-Deans body could listen as well
as give out. We are told that it was not so much that
she said brilliant things, but that a general perfume of
wit ran through her conversation, and she most certainly
had the gift of appreciating the good things of others.
Whether in that ' scene of simplicity, truth, and nature '
a London rout, or in some quiet Hampstead parlour talking to an old friend, or in her own home among books and
relations and interests of every sort, Miss Edgeworth
seems to have been constantly the same, with presence of
mind and presence of heart too, ready to respond to everything. I think her warmth of heart shines even brighter
than her wit at times. ' I could not bear the idea that
you suspected me of being so weak, so vain, so senseless,'
she once wrote to Mrs. Barbauld, ' as to have my head
turned by a little fashionable flattery.' If her head was
not turned it must have been because her spirit was stout
enough to withstand the world's almost irresistible
influence.

Not only the great men but the women too are among her friends. She writes prettily of Mrs. Somerville, with her smiling eyes and pink colour, her soft voice, strong, well-bred Scotch accent, timid, not disqualifying timid, but naturally modest. 'While her head is among the stars her feet are firm upon the earth.' She is 'delighted' with a criticism of Madame de Staël's upon herself, in a letter to M. Dumont. 'Vraiment elle était digne de l'enthousiasme, mais elle se perd dans votre triste utilité.' It is difficult to understand why this should have given Miss Edgeworth so much pleasure; and here finally is a little vision conjured up for us of her meeting with Mrs. Fry among her prisoners:—

Little doors, and thick doors, and doors of all sorts were unbolted and unlocked, and on we went through dreary but clean passages till we came to a room where rows of empty benches fronted us, a table on which lay a large Bible. Several ladies and gentlemen entered, took their seats on benches at either side of the table in silence. Enter Mrs. Fry in a drab-coloured silk cloak and a plain, borderless Quaker cap, a most benevolent countenance, calm, benign. 'I must make an inquiry. Is Maria Edgeworth here?' And when I went forward she bade me come and sit beside her. Her first smile as she looked upon me I can never forget. The prisoners came in in an orderly manner and ranged themselves upon the benches.

## XV.

' In this my sixtieth year, to commence in a few days,' says Miss Edgeworth, writing to her cousin Margaret Ruxton, ' I am resolved to make great progress.' ' Rosamond at sixty,' says Miss Ruxton, touched and amused. Her resolutions were not idle.

' The universal difficulties of the money market in the year 1826 were felt by us,' says Mrs. Edgeworth in her memoir, ' and Maria, who since her father's death had given up rent-receiving, now resumed it ; undertook the management of her brother Lovell's affairs, which she conducted with consummate skill and perseverance, and weathered the storm that swamped so many in this financial crisis.' We also hear of an opportune windfall in the shape of some valuable diamonds, which an old lady, a distant relation, left in her will to Miss Edgeworth, who sold them and built a market-house for Edgeworthtown with the proceeds.

*April* 8, 1827.—I am quite well and in high good humour and good spirits, in consequence of having received the whole of Lovell's half-year's rents in full, with pleasure to the tenants and without the least fatigue or anxiety to myself.

It was about this time her novel of ' Helen ' was written, the last of her books, the only one that her father had not revised. There is a vivid account given by one of her brothers of the family assembled in the library to hear the manuscript read out, of their anxiety and their pleasure as they realised how good it was, how spirited, how well equal to her standard. Tickner, in his account of Miss Edgeworth, says that the talk of Lady Davenant in 'Helen' is very like Miss Edgeworth's own manner. His visit to Edgeworthtown was not long after the publication of the book. His description, if only for her mention of her father, is worth quoting :—

As we drove to the door Miss Edgeworth came out to meet us, a small, short, spare body of about sixty-seven, with extremely frank and kind manners, but who always looks straight into your face with a pair of mild deep grey eyes whenever she speaks to you. With characteristic directness she did not take us into the library until she had told us that we should find there Mrs. Alison, of Edinburgh, and her aunt, Miss Sneyd, a person very old and infirm, and that the only other persons constituting the family were Mrs. Edgeworth, Miss Honora Edgeworth, and Dr. Alison, a physician. . . . Miss Edgeworth's conversation was always ready, as full of vivacity and variety as I can imagine. . . . She was disposed to defend everybody, even Lady Morgan, as far as she could. And in her intercourse with her family she was quite delightful, referring constantly to Mrs. Edgeworth, who seems to be the authority in all matters of fact, and most kindly repeating jokes to her infirm aunt, Miss Sneyd, who cannot hear them, and who seems to have for her the most unbounded affection and admiration. . . . About herself as an author she seems to have no reserve or secrets. She spoke with

L

great kindness and pleasure of a letter I brought to her from Mr. Peabody, explaining some passage in his review of ' Helen ' which had troubled her from its allusion to her father. ' But,' she added, ' no one can know what I owe to my father. He advised and directed me in everything. I never could have done anything without him. There are things I cannot be mistaken about, though other people can. I know them.' As she said this the tears stood in her eyes, and her whole person was moved. . . . It was, therefore, something of a trial to talk so brilliantly and variously as she did from nine in the morning to past eleven at night.

She was unfeignedly glad to see good company. Here is her account of another visitor :—

*Sept.* 26.—The day before yesterday we were amusing ourselves by telling who among literary and scientific people we should wish to come here next. Francis said Coleridge ; I said Herschell. Yesterday morning, as I was returning from my morning walk at half-past eight, I saw a bonnetless maid in the walk, with a letter in her hand, in search of me. When I opened the letter I found it was from Mr. Herschell, and that he was waiting for an answer at Mr. Briggs's inn. I have seldom been so agreeably surprised, and now that he is gone and that he has spent twenty-four hours here, if the fairy were to ask me the question again I should still more eagerly say, ' Mr. Herschell, ma'am, if you please.'

She still came over to England from time to time, visiting at her sisters' houses. Honora was now Lady Beaufort ; another sister, Fanny, the object of her closest and most tender affection, was Mrs. Lestock Wilson. Age brought no change in her mode of life. Time passes with tranquil steps, for her not hasting unduly. 'I am perfect,' she writes at the age of seventy-three to her stepmother of seventy-two, 'so no more about it, and thank you from my heart and every component part of my precious self for all the care, and successful care, you have taken of me, your old petted nurseling.'

Alas! it is sad to realise that quite late in life fresh sorrows fell upon this warm-hearted woman. Troubles gather; young sisters fade away in their beauty and happiness. But in sad times and good times the old home is still unchanged, and remains for those that are left to turn to for shelter, for help, and consolation. To the very last Miss Edgeworth kept up her reading, her correspondence, her energy. All along we have heard of her active habits—out in the early morning in her garden, coming in to the nine o'clock breakfast with her hands full of roses, sitting by and talking and reading her letters while the others ate. Her last letter to her old friend Sir Henry Holland was after reading the first volume of Lord Macaulay's History. Sir Henry took the letter to Lord Macaulay, who was so much struck by its discrimination that he asked leave to keep it.

She was now eighty-two years of age, and we find her laughing kindly at the anxiety of her sister and brother-

in-law, who had heard of her climbing a ladder to wind up
an old clock at Edgeworthtown. ' I am heartily obliged
and delighted by your being such a goose and Richard
such a gander,' she says ' as to be frightened out of your
wits by my climbing a ladder to take off the top of the
clock.' She had not felt that there was anything to fear
as once again she set the time that was so nearly at an
end for her. Her share of life's hours had been well spent
and well enjoyed ; with a peaceful and steady hand and
tranquil heart she might mark the dial for others whose
hours were still to come.

Mrs. Edgeworth's own words tell all that remains to be
told.

It was on the morning of May 22, 1849, that she was
taken suddenly ill with pain in the region of the heart, and
after a few hours breathed her last in my arms. She had
always wished to die quickly, at home, and that I should be
with her. All her wishes were fulfilled. She was gone, and
nothing like her again can we see in this world.

# MRS OPIE.

## 1769–1853.

' Your gentleness shall force more than your force move us to gentleness.'—*As You Like It*.

## I.

It is not very long since some articles appeared in the ' Cornhill Magazine ' which were begun under the influence of certain ancient bookshelves with so pleasant a flavour of the old world that it seemed at the time as if yesterday not to-day was the all-important hour, and one gladly submitted to the subtle charm of the past—its silent veils, its quiet incantations of dust and healing cobweb. The phase is but a passing one with most of us, and we must soon feel that to dwell at length upon each one of the pretty old fancies and folios of the writers and explorers who were born towards the end of the last century would be an impossible affectation; and yet a postscript seems wanting to the sketches which have already appeared of Mrs. Barbauld and Miss Edgeworth, and the names of their contemporaries should not be quite passed over.

In a hundred charming types and prints and portraits
we recognise the well-known names as they used to appear
in the garb of life.  Grand ladies in broad loops and
feathers, or graceful and charming as nymphs in muslin
folds, with hanging clouds of hair ; or again, in modest
coiffes such as dear Jane Austen loved and wore even in her
youth.  Hannah More only took to coiffes and wimples in
later life ; in early days she was fond of splendour, and,
as we read, had herself painted in emerald earrings.  How
many others besides her are there to admire !  Who does
not know the prim, sweet, amply frilled portraits of Mrs.
Trimmer and Joanna Baillie ?  Only yesterday a friend
showed me a sprightly, dark-eyed miniature of Felicia
Hemans.  Perhaps most beautiful among all her sister
muses smiles the lovely head of Amelia Opie, as she was
represented by her husband with luxuriant chestnut hair
piled up Romney fashion in careless loops, with the radiant
yet dreaming eyes which are an inheritance for some
members of her family.

The authoresses of that day had the pre-eminence in
looks, in gracious dress and bearing ; but they were rather
literary women than anything else, and had but little in common with the noble and brilliant writers who were to follow
them in our own more natural and outspoken times ; whose
wise, sweet, passionate voices are already passing away into

the distance ; of whom so few remain to us.[1] The secret of being real is no very profound one, and yet how rare it is, how long it was before the readers and writers of this century found it out! It is like the secret of singing in perfect tune, or of playing the violin as Joachim can play upon it. In literature, as in music, there is at times a certain indescribable tone of absolute reality which carries the reader away and for the moment absorbs him into the mind of the writer. Some metempsychosis takes place. It is no longer a man or a woman turning the pages of a book, it is a human being suddenly absorbed by the book itself, living the very life which it records, breathing the spirit and soul of the writer. Such books are events, not books to us, new conditions of existence, new selves suddenly revealed through the experience of other more vivid personalities than our own. The actual experience of other lives is not for us, but this link of simple reality of feeling is one all independent of events ; it is like the miracle of the loaves and fishes repeated and multiplied—one man comes with his fishes and lo ! the multitude is filled.

But this simple discovery, that of reality, that of speaking from the heart, was one of the last to be made

[1] And yet as I write I remember one indeed who is among us, whose portrait a Reynolds or an Opie might have been glad to paint for the generations who will love her works.

by women. In France Madame de Sévigné and Madame de La Fayette were not afraid to be themselves, but in England the majority of authoresses kept their readers carefully at pen's length, and seemed for the most part to be so conscious of their surprising achievements in the way of literature as never to forget for a single instant that they were in print. With the exception of Jane Austen and Maria Edgeworth, the women writers of the early part of this century were, as I have just said, rather literary women than actual creators of literature. It is still a mystery how they attained to their great successes. Frances Burney charms great Burke and mighty Johnson and wise Macaulay in later times. Mrs. Opie draws compliments from Mackintosh, and compliments from the Duchess of Saxe-Coburg, and Sydney Smith, and above all tears from Walter Scott.

Perhaps many of the flattering things addressed to Mrs. Opie may have said not less for her own charm and sweetness of nature than for the merit of her unassuming productions ; she must have been a bright, merry, and fascinating person, and compliments were certainly more in her line than the tributes of tears which she records.

The authoresses of heroines are often more interesting than the heroines themselves, and Amelia Opie was certainly no exception to this somewhat general statement. A pleasant, sprightly authoress, beaming bright glances on her friends, confident, intelligent, full of interest in life, carried along in turn by one and by another influence, she comes before us a young and charming figure, with all the spires of Norwich for a background, and the sound of its bells, and the stir of its assizes, as she issues from her peaceful home in her father's tranquil old house, where the good physician lives widowed, tending his poor and his sick, and devotedly spoiling his only child.

## II.

Amelia Opie was born in 1769 in the old city of Norwich, within reach of the invigorating breezes of the great North Sea. Her youth must have been somewhat solitary; she was the only child of a kind and cultivated physician, Doctor James Alderson, whose younger brother, a barrister, also living in Norwich, became the father of Baron Alderson. Her mother died in her early youth. From her father, however, little Amelia seems to have had the love and indulgence of over half a century, a tender and admiring love which she returned with all her heart's devotion. She was the pride and darling of his home, and throughout her long life her father's approbation was the one chief motive of her existence. Spoiling is a vexed question, but as a rule people get so much stern justice from all the rest of the world that it seems well that their parents should love and comfort them in youth for the many disgraces and difficulties yet to come.

Her mother is described as a delicate, high-minded woman, 'somewhat of a disciplinarian,' says Mrs. Opie's excellent biographer, Miss Brightwell, but she died too soon to carry her theories into practice. Miss Brightwell suggests that 'Mrs. Opie might have been more demure and decorous had her mother lived, but perhaps less charming.' There are some verses addressed to her mother in Mrs. Opie's papers in which it must be confessed that the remembrance of her admonition plays a most important part—

> Hark ! clearer still thy voice I hear.
> Again reproof in accents mild,
> Seems whispering in my conscious ear,

and so on.

Some of Mrs. Alderson's attempts at discipline seemed unusual and experimental; the little girl was timid, afraid of black people, of black beetles, and of human skeletons. She was given the skeleton to play with, and the beetles to hold in her hand. One feels more sympathy with the way in which she was gently reconciled to the poor negro with the frightening black face—by being told the story of his wrongs. But with the poor mother's untimely death all this maternal supervision came to an end. 'Amelia, your mother is gone ; may you never have reason to blush when you remember her!' her father said as he clasped his little orphan to his heart ; and all her life long Amelia remembered those words.

There is a pretty reminiscence of her childhood from a beginning of the memoir which was never written :— 'One of my earliest recollections is of gazing on the bright blue sky as I lay in my little bed before my hour of rising came, listening with delighted attention to the ringing of a peal of bells. I had heard that heaven was beyond those blue skies, and I had been taught that *there* was the home of the good, and I fancied that those sweet bells were ringing in heaven.' The bells were ringing for the Norwich Assizes, which played an important part in our little heroine's life, and which must have been associated with many of her early memories.

The little girl seems to have been allowed more liberty than is usually given to children. 'As soon as I was old enough to enjoy a procession,' she says, 'I was taken to see the Judges come in. Youthful pages in pretty dresses ran by the side of the High Sheriff's carriage, in which the Judges sat, while the coaches drove slowly and with a solemnity becoming the high and awful office of those whom they contained. . . . . With reverence ever did I behold the Judges' wigs, the scarlet robes they wore, and even the white wand of the Sheriff.'

There is a description which in after years might have made a pretty picture for her husband's pencil of the little maiden wandering into the court one day, and called by a kind old Judge to sit beside him upon the bench. She goes on to recount how next day she was there again ; and when some attendant of the court wanted her to leave the place, saying not unnaturally, 'Go, Miss, this is no place for you ; be advised,' the Judge again interfered, and ordered the enterprising little girl to be brought to her old place upon the cushion by his side. The story gives one a curious impression of a child's life and education. She seems to have come and gone alone, capable, intelligent, unabashed, interested in all the events and humours of the place.

Children have among other things a very vivid sense of citizenship and public spirit, somewhat put out in later life by the rush of personal feeling, but in childhood the personal events are so few and so irresponsible that public affairs become an actual part of life and of experience. While their elders are still discussing the news and weighing its importance, it is already a part of the children's life. Little Amelia Alderson must have been a happy child, free, affectionate, independent; grateful, as a child should be, towards those who befriended her. One of her teachers was a French dancing-master called Christian, for whom she had a warm regard. She relates that long afterwards she came with her husband and a friend to visit the Dutch church at Norwich. ' The two gentlemen were engaged in looking round and making their observations, and I, finding myself somewhat cold, began to hop and dance upon the spot where I stood, when my eyes chanced to fall upon the pavement below, and I started at beholding the well-known name of Christian graved upon the slab; I stopped in dismay, shocked to find that I had actually been dancing upon the grave of my old master—he who first taught me to dance.'

### III.

After her mother's death, Amelia Alderson, who was barely fifteen at the time, began to take her place in society. She kept her father's house, received his friends, made his home bright with her presence. The lawyers came round in due season : Sir James Mackintosh came, the town was full of life, of talk, of music, and poetry, and prejudice.

Harriet Martineau, in her memoir of Mrs. Opie, gives a delightful and humorous account of the Norwich of that day—rivalling Lichfield and its literary coterie, only with less sentimentality and some additional peculiarities of its own. One can almost see the Tory gentlemen, as Miss Martineau describes them, setting a watch upon the Cathedral, lest the Dissenters should burn it as a beacon for Boney ; whereas good Bishop Bathurst, with more faith in human nature, goes on resolutely touching his hat to the leading Nonconformists. ' The French taught in schools,' says Miss Martineau, ' was found to be unintelligible when the peace at length arrived, taught as it was by an aged powdered Monsieur and an elderly flowered Madame, who had taught their pupils' Norfolk pronunciation. But it was beginning to be known,' she continues, ' that there was such a language as German, and in due time there was a young man who had actually been in Germany, and was translating " Nathan the Wise." When William Taylor became eminent as almost the only German scholar in England, old Norwich was very proud and grew, to say the truth, excessively conceited. She was (and she might be) proud of her Sayers, she boasted of her intellectual supper-parties, and finally called herself the " Athens of England." '

In this wholesome, cheerful Athens, blown by the invigorating Northern breezes, little Amelia bloomed and developed into a lovely and happy girl. She was fortunate, indeed, in her friends. One near at hand must have been an invaluable adviser for a motherless, impressionable girl.

Mrs. John Taylor was so loved that she is still remembered. Mrs. Barbauld prized and valued her affection beyond all others. 'I know the value of your letters,' says Sir James Mackintosh, writing from Bombay ; 'they rouse my mind on subjects which interest us in common— children, literature, and life. I ought to be made permanently better by contemplating a mind like yours.' And he still has Mrs. Taylor in his mind when he concludes with a little disquisition on the contrast between the barren sensibility, the indolent folly of some, the useful kindness of others, 'the industrious benevolence which requires a vigorous understanding and a decisive character.'

Some of Mrs. Opie's family have shown me a photograph of her in her Quaker dress, in old age, dim, and changed, and sunken, from which it is very difficult to realise all the brightness, and life, and animation which must have belonged to the earlier part of her life. The delightful portrait of her engraved in the 'Mirror' shows the animated beaming countenance, the soft expressive eyes, the abundant auburn waves of hair, of which we read. The picture is more like some charming allegorical being than a real live young lady—some Belinda of the 'Rape of the Lock' (and one would as soon have expected Belinda to turn Quakeress). Music, poetry, dancing, elves, graces and flirtations, cupids, seem to attend her steps. She delights in admiration, friendship, companionship, and gaiety, and yet with it all we realise a warm-hearted sincerity, and appreciation of good and high-minded things, a truth of feeling passing out of the realms of fancy altogether into one of the best realities of life. She had a thousand links with life : she was musical, artistic ; she was literary ; she had a certain amount of social influence ; she had a voice, a harp, a charming person, mind and manner. Admiring monarchs in later days applauded her performance ; devoted subjects were her friends and correspondents, and her sphere in due time extended beyond the approving Norwich-Athenian coterie of old friends who had known her from her childhood, to London itself, where she seems to have been made welcome by many, and to have captivated more than her share of victims.

In some letters of hers written to Mrs. Taylor and quoted by her biographer we get glimpses of some of these early experiences. The bright and happy excitable girl comes up from Norwich to London to be made more happy still, and more satisfied with the delight of life as it unfolds. Besides her fancy for lawyers, literary people had a great attraction for Amelia, and Godwin seems to have played an important part in her earlier experience. A saying of Mrs. Inchbald's is quoted by her on her retnrn home as to the report of the world being that Mr. Holcroft was in love with Mrs. Inchbald, Mrs. Inchbald with Mr. Godwin, Mr. Godwin with Miss Alderson, and Miss Alderson with Mr. Holcroft!

The following account of Somers Town, and a philosopher's costume in those days, is written to her father in 1794 :—

After a most delightful ride through some of the richest country I ever beheld, we arrived about one o'clock at the philosopher's house; we found him with his hair *bien poudré*, and in a pair of new sharp-toed red morocco slippers, not to mention his green coat and crimson under-waistcoat.

From Godwin's by the city they come to Marlborough Street, and find Mrs. Siddons nursing her little baby, and as handsome and charming as ever. They see Charles Kemble there, and they wind up their day by calling on Mrs. Inchbald in her pleasant lodgings, with two hundred pounds just come in from Sheridan for a farce of sixty pages. Godwin's attentions seem to have amused and pleased the fair, merry Amelia, who is not a little proud of her arch influence over various rugged and apparently inaccessible persons. Mrs. Inchbald seems to have been as jealous of Miss Alderson at the time as she afterwards was of Mary Wollstonecraft. 'Will you give me nothing to keep for your sake?' says Godwin, parting from Amelia. 'Not even your slipper? I had it once in my possession.'

M

' This was true,' adds Miss Amelia; ' my shoe had come
off and he picked it up and put it in his pocket.' Elsewhere she tells her friend Mrs. Taylor that Mr. Holcroft
would like to come forward, but that he had no chance.

That some one person had a chance, and a very good
one, is plain enough from the context of a letter, but
there is nothing in Mrs. Opie's life to show why fate was
contrary in this, while yielding so bountiful a share of all
other good things to the happy country girl.

Among other people, she seems to have charmed
various French refugees, one of whom was the Duc
d'Aiguillon, come over to England with some seven
thousand others, waiting here for happier times, and
hiding their sorrows among our friendly mists. Godwin
was married when Miss Alderson revisited her London
friends and admirers in 1797—an eventful visit, when she
met Opie for the first time.

The account of their first meeting is amusingly given
in Miss Brightwell's memoirs. It was at an evening
party. Some of those present were eagerly expecting
the arrival of Miss Alderson, but the evening was wearing
away and still she did not appear; ' at length the door was
flung open, and she entered bright and smiling, dressed
in a robe of blue, her neck and arms bare, and on her
head a small bonnet placed in somewhat coquettish style

sideways and surmounted by a plume of three white
feathers. Her beautiful hair hung in waving tresses over
her shoulders ; her face was kindling with pleasure at the
sight of her old friends, and her whole appearance was
animated and glowing. At the time she came in Mr.
Opie was sitting on a sofa beside Mr. F., who had been
saying from time to time, 'Amelia is coming; Amelia will
surely come. Why is she not here?' and whose eyes were
turned in her direction. He was interrupted by her companion eagerly exclaiming, 'Who is that—who is that?'
and hastily rising Opie pressed forward to be introduced
to the fair object whose sudden appearance had so
impressed him.' With all her love of excitement, of
change, of variety, one cannot but feel, as I have said,
that there was also in Amelia Alderson's cheerful life a
vein of deep and very serious feeling, and the bracing
influence of the upright and high-minded people among
whom she had been brought up did not count for nothing
in her nature. She could show her genuine respect for
what was generous and good and true, even though she
did not always find strength to carry out the dream of an
excitable and warm-hearted nature.

### IV.

There is something very interesting in the impression
one receives of the ' Inspired Peasant,' as Alan Cunningham
calls John Opie—the man who did not paint to live so
much as live to paint.  He was a simple, high-minded
Cornishman, whose natural directness and honesty were
unspoiled by favour, unembittered by failure.  Opie's gift,
like some deep-rooted seed living buried in arid soil, ever
aspired upwards towards the light.  His ideal was high;
his performance fell far short of his life-long dream, and
he knew it.  But his heart never turned from its life's
aim, and he loved beauty and Art with that true and unfailing devotion which makes a man great, even though his
achievements do not show all he should have been.

The old village carpenter, his father, who meant him
to succeed to the business, was often angry, and loudly
railed at the boy when good white-washed walls and clean
boards were spoiled by scrawls of lamp-black and charcoal.
John worked in the shop and obeyed his father, but when his
day's task was over he turned again to his darling pursuits.
At twelve years old he had mastered Euclid, and could also
rival ' Mark Oaks,' the village phenomenon, in painting a
butterfly ; by the time John was sixteen he could earn as

much as 7*s*. 6*d*. for a portrait. It was in this year that there came to Truro an accomplished and various man Dr. Wolcott—sometimes a parson, sometimes a doctor of medicine, sometimes as Peter Pindar, a critic and literary man. This gentleman was interested by young Opie and his performances, and he asked him on one occasion how he liked painting. ' Better than bread-and-butter,' says the boy. Wolcott finally brought his *protégé* to London, where the Doctor's influence and Opie's own undoubted merit brought him success; and to Opie's own amazement he suddenly found himself the fashion. His street was crowded with carriages; long processions of ladies and gentlemen came to sit to him; he was able to furnish a house 'in Orange Court, by Leicester Fields;' he was beginning to put by money when, as suddenly as he had been taken up, he was forgotten again. The carriages drove off in some other direction, and Opie found himself abandoned by the odd, fanciful world of fashions, which would not be fashions if they did not change day by day. It might have proved a heart-breaking phase of life for a man whose aim had been less single. But Opie was of too generous a nature to value popularity beyond achievement. He seems to have borne this freak of fortune with great equanimity, and when he was sometimes overwhelmed, it was not by the praise or dispraise of others, but by his own consciousness of failure, of inadequate performance. Troubles even more serious than loss of patronage and employment befell him later. He had married, unhappily for himself, a beautiful, unworthy woman, whose picture he has painted many times. She was a faithless as well as a weak and erring wife, and finally abandoned him. When Opie was free to marry again he was thirty-six, a serious, downright man of undoubted power and influence, of sincerity and tenderness of feeling, of rugged and unusual manners. He had not many friends, nor did he wish for many, but those who knew him valued him at his worth. His second wife showed what was in her by her appreciation of his noble qualities, though one can hardly realise a greater contrast than that of these two, so unlike in character, in training, and disposition. They were married in London, at Marylebone Church, in that dismal year of '98, which is still remembered. Opie loved his wife deeply and passionately; he did not charm her, though she charmed him, but for his qualities she had true respect and admiration.

## V.

Opie must be forgiven if he was one-idead, if he erred from too much zeal. All his wife's bright gaiety of nature, her love for her fellow-creatures, her interest in the world, her many-sidedness, this uncompromising husband would gladly have kept for himself. For him his wife and his home were the whole world; his Art was his whole life.

The young couple settled down in London after their marriage, where, notwithstanding fogs and smoke and dull monotony of brick and smut, so many beautiful things are created; where Turner's rainbow lights were first reflected, where Tennyson's ' Princess ' sprang from the fog. It was a modest and quiet installation, but among the pretty things which Amelia brought to brighten her new home we read of blue feathers and gold gauze bonnets, tiaras, and spencers, scarlet ribbons, buff net, and cambric flounces, all of which give one a pleasant impression of her intention to amuse herself, and to enjoy the society of her fellows, and to bring her own pleasant contributions to their enjoyment.

Opie sat working at his easel, painting portraits to earn money for his wife's use and comfort, and encouraging her to write, for he had faith in work. He himself would never intermit his work for a single day. He would have gladly kept her always in his sight. ' If I would stay at home for ever, I believe my husband would be merry from morning to night—a lover more than a husband,' Amelia writes to Mrs. Taylor. He seemed to have some feeling that time for him was not to be long—that life was passing quickly by, almost too quickly to give him time to realise his new home happiness, to give him strength to grasp his work. He was no rapid painter, instinctively feeling his light and colour and action, and seizing the moment's suggestion, but anxious, laborious, and involved in that sad struggle in which some people pass their lives, for ever disappointed. Opie's portraits seem to have been superior to his compositions, which were well painted, ' but unimaginative and commonplace,' says a painter of our own time, whose own work quickens with that mysterious soul which some pictures (as indeed some human beings) seem to be entirely without.

' During the nine years that I was his wife,' says Mrs. Opie, ' I never saw him satisfied with any one of his productions. Often, very often, he has entered my sitting-room, and, throwing himself down in an agony of despondence upon the sofa, exclaimed, " I shall never be a painter ! " '

He was a wise and feeling critic, however great his shortcomings as a painter may have been. His lectures are admirable ; full of real thought and good judgment. Sir James Mackintosh places them beyond Reynolds's in some ways.

' If there were no difficulties every one would be a painter,' says Opie, and he goes on to point out what a painter's object should be—' the discovery or conception of perfect ideas of things; nature in its purest and most essential form rising from the species to the genus, the highest and ultimate exertion of human genius.' For him it was no grievance that a painter's life should be one long and serious effort. ' If you are wanting to your-selves, rule may be multiplied upon rule and precept upon precept in vain.' Some of his remarks might be thought still to apply in many cases, no less than they did a hundred years ago, when he complained of those green-sick lovers of chalk, brick-dust, charcoal and old tapestry, who are so ready to decry the merits of colouring and to set it down as a kind of superfluity. It is curious to contrast Opie's style in literature with that of his wife, who belongs to the entirely past generation which she reflected, whereas he wrote from his own original impres-sions, saying those things which struck him as forcibly then as they strike us now. ' Father and Daughter ' was Mrs. Opie's first acknowledged book. It was published in 1801, and the author writes modestly of all her apprehen-sions. ' Mr. Opie has no patience with me ; he consoles me by averring that fear makes me overrate others and underrate myself.' The book was reviewed in the ' Edin-burgh.' We hear of one gentleman who lies awake all night after reading it ; and Mrs. Inchbald promises a candid opinion, which, however, we do not get. Besides stories and novels, Mrs. Opie was the author of several poems and verses which were much admired. There was an impromptu to Sir James Mackintosh, which brought a long letter in return, and one of her songs was quoted by Sydney Smith in a lecture at the Royal Institution. Mrs. Opie was present, and she used to tell in after times ' how unexpectedly the compliment came upon her, and how she shrunk down upon her seat in order to screen herself from observation.'

The lines are indeed charming :—

> Go, youth, beloved in distant glades,
>     New friends, new hopes, new joys to find,
> Yet sometimes deign 'midst fairer maids
>     To think on her thou leav'st behind.
> Thy love, thy fate, dear youth to share
>     Must never be my happy lot;
> But thou may'st grant this humble prayer,
>     Forget me not, forget me not.
>
> Yet should the thought of my distress
>     Too painful to thy feelings be,
> Heed not the wish I now express,
>     Nor ever deign to think of me;
> But oh ! if grief thy steps attend,
>     If want, if sickness be thy lot,
> And thou require a soothing friend,
>     Forget me not, forget me not.

## VI.

The little household was a modest one, but we read of a certain amount of friendly hospitality. Country neighbours from Norfolk appear upon the scene; we find Northcote dining and praising the toasted cheese. Mrs. Opie's heart never for an instant ceased to warm to her old friends and companions. She writes an amusing account to Mrs. Taylor of her London home, her interests and visitors, 'her happy and delightful life.' She worked, she amused herself, she received her friends at home and went to look for them abroad. Among other visits, Mrs. Opie speaks of one to an old friend who has 'grown plump,' and of a second to ' Betsy Fry ' who, notwithstanding her comfortable home and prosperous circumstances, has grown lean. It would be difficult to recognise under this familiar cognomen and description the noble and dignified woman whose name and work are still remembered with affectionate respect and wonder by a not less hard-working, but less convinced and convincing generation. This friendship was of great moment to Amelia Opie in after days, at a time when her heart was low and her life very sad and solitary; but meanwhile, as I have said, there were happy times for her; youth and youthful spirits and faithful companionship were all hers, and troubles had not yet come.

One day Mrs. Opie gives a characteristic account of a visit from Mrs. Taylor's two sons. ' " John," said I, " will you take a letter from me to your mother ? " " Certainly," replied John, " for then I shall be sure of being welcome." " Fy," returned I. " Mr. Courtier, you know you want nothing to add to the heartiness of the welcome you will receive at home." " No, indeed," said Richard, " and if Mrs. Opie sends her letter by you it will be one way of making it less valued and attended to than it would otherwise be." To the truth of this speech I subscribed and wrote not. I have heard in later days a pretty description of the simple home in which all these handsome, cultivated, and remarkable young people grew up round their noble-minded mother.' One of Mrs. John Taylor's daughters became Mrs. Reeve, the mother of Mr. Henry Reeve, another was Mrs. Austin, the mother of Lady Duff Gordon.

Those lean kine we read of in the Bible are not peculiar to Egypt and to the days of Joseph and his brethren. The unwelcome creatures are apt to make their appearance in many a country and many a household, and in default of their natural food to devour all sorts of long-cherished fancies, hopes, and schemes. Some time after his marriage, Opie suddenly, and for no reason, found himself without employment, and the severest trial they experienced during their married life, says his wife, was during this period of anxiety. She, however, cheered him womanfully, would not acknowledge her own dismay, and Opie, gloomy and desponding though he was, continued to paint as regularly as before. Presently orders began to flow in again, and did not cease until his death.

## VII.

Their affairs being once more prosperous, a long-hoped-for dream became a reality, and they started on an expedition to Paris, a solemn event in those days and not lightly to be passed over by a biographer. One long war was ended, another had not yet begun. The Continent was a promised land, fondly dreamt of though unknown. 'At last in Paris; at last in the city which she had so longed to see!' Mrs. Opie's description of her arrival reads a comment upon history. As they drive into the town, everywhere chalked up upon the walls and the houses are inscriptions concerning 'L'Indivisibilité de la République.' How many subsequent writings upon the wall did Mrs. Opie live to see! The English party find rooms at a hotel facing the Place de la Concorde, where the guillotine, that token of order and tranquillity, was then

perpetually standing. The young wife's feelings may be
imagined when within an hour of their arrival Opie, who
had rushed off straight to the Louvre, returned with a
face of consternation to say that they must leave Paris at
once. The Louvre was shut ; and, moreover, the whiteness
of everything, the houses, the ground they stood on, all
dazzled and blinded him. He was a lost man if he remained ! By some happy interposition they succeed in
getting admission to the Louvre, and as the painter
wonders and admires his nervous terrors leave him. The
picture left by Miss Edgeworth of Paris Society in the
early years of the century is more brilliant, but not more
interesting than Mrs. Opie's reminiscences of the fleeting
scene, gaining so much in brilliancy from the shadows all
round about. There is the shadow of the ghastly
guillotine upon the Place de la Concorde, the shadows of
wars but lately over and yet to come, the echo in the air
of arms and discord ; meanwhile a brilliant, agreeable,
flashing Paris streams with sunlight, is piled with treasures
and trophies of victory, and crowded with well-known
characters. We read of Kosciusko's nut-brown wig con-
cealing his honourable scars ; Masséna's earrings flash in
the sun ; one can picture it all, and the animated inrush
of tourists, and the eager life stirring round about the
walls of the old Louvre.

It was at this time that they saw Talma perform, and
years after, in her little rooms in Lady's Field at Norwich,
Mrs. Opie, in her Quaker dress, used to give an imitation
of the great actor and utter a deep ' Cain, Cain, where art
thou ? ' To which Cain replies in sepulchral tones.

We get among other things an interesting glimpse of
Fox standing in the Louvre Gallery opposite the picture
of St. Jerome by Domenichino, a picture which, as it is
said, he enthusiastically admired. Opie, who happened to
be introduced to him, then and there dissented from this
opinion. ' You must be a better judge on such points
than I am,' says Fox; and Mrs. Opie proudly writes of
the two passing on together discussing and comparing the
pictures. She describes them next standing before the
' Transfiguration ' of Raphael. The Louvre in those days
must have been for a painter a wonder palace indeed. The
' Venus de' Medici ' was on her way; it was a time of
miracles, as Fox said. Meanwhile Mrs. Opie hears some-
one saying that the First Consul is on his way from the
Senate, and she hurries to a window to look out. ' Bonaparte
seems very fond of state and show for a Republican,' says
Mrs. Fox. Fox himself half turns to the window, then
looks back to the pictures again. As for Opie, one may be
sure his attention never wandered for one instant.

They saw the First Consul more than once. The

Pacificator, as he was then called, was at the height of his
popularity; on one occasion they met Fox with his wife on
his arm crossing the Carrousel to the Tuileries, where they
are also admitted to a ground-floor room, from whence they
look upon a marble staircase and see several officers ascending, ' one of whom, with a helmet which seemed entirely
of gold, was Eugène de Beauharnais. A few minutes
afterwards,' she says, ' there was a rush of officers down
the stairs, and among them I saw a short pale man with
his hat in his hand, who, as I thought, resembled Lord
Erskine in profile. . . .' This of course is Bonaparte,
unadorned amidst all this studied splendour, and wearing
only a little tricoloured cockade. Maria Cosway, the
painter, who was also in Paris at the time, took them to
call at the house of Madame Bonaparte *mère*, where they
were received by ' a blooming, courteous ecclesiastic,
powdered and with purple stockings and gold buckles, and
a costly crucifix. This is Cardinal Fesch, the uncle of
Bonaparte. It is said that when Fox was introduced to
the First Consul he was warmly welcomed by him, and
was made to listen to a grand harangue upon the ad-
vantages of peace, to which he answered scarcely a word;
though he was charmed to talk with Madame Bonaparte,
and to discuss with her the flowers of which she was so
fond.' The Opies met Fox again in England some years

after, when he sat to Opie for one of his finest portraits.
It is now at Holker, and there is a characteristic description
of poor Opie, made nervous by the criticism of the many
friends, and Fox, impatient but encouraging, and again
whispering, ' Don't attend to them ; you must know best.'


## VIII.

' Adeline Mowbray; or, Mother and Daughter,' was
published by Mrs. Opie after this visit to the Continent.
It is a melancholy and curious story, which seems to have
been partly suggested by that of poor Mary Wollstonecraft,
whose prejudices the heroine shares and expiates by a fate
hardly less pathetic than that of Mary herself. The book
reminds one of a very touching letter from Godwin's wife
to Amelia Alderson, written a few weeks before her death,
in which she speaks of her ' contempt for the forms of a
world she should have bade a long good-night to had she
not been a mother.' Justice has at length been done to
this mistaken but noble and devoted woman, and her story
has lately been written from a wider point of view than
Mrs. Opie's, though she indeed was no ungenerous advocate.
Her novel seems to have given satisfaction; ' a beautiful
story, the most natural in its pathos of any fictitious
narrative in the language,' says the ' Edinburgh, writing

N

with more leniency than authors now expect. Another
reviewer, speaking with discriminating criticism, says of
Mrs. Opie : ' She does not reason well, but she has, like
most accomplished women, the talent of perceiving truth
without the process of reasoning. Her language is often
inaccurate, but it is always graceful and harmonious. She
can do nothing well that requires to be done with formality ;
to make amends, however, she represents admirably everything that is amiable, generous, and gentle.'

Adeline Mowbray dies of a broken heart, with the following somewhat discursive farewell to her child : ' There
are two ways in which a mother can be of use to her
daughter ; the one is by instilling into her mind virtuous
principles, and by setting her a virtuous example, the other
is by being to her, in her own person, an awful warning ! '

One or two of Opie's letters to his wife are given in
the memoir. They ring with truth and tender feeling.
The two went to Norwich together on one occasion, when
Opie painted Dr. Sayers, the scholar, who, in return for
his portrait, applied an elegant Greek distich to the
painter. Mrs. Opie remained with her father, and her
husband soon returned to his studio in London. When
she delayed, he wrote to complain. ' My dearest Life, I
cannot be sorry that you do not stay longer, though, as I

said, on your father's account, I would consent to it. Pray, Love, forgive me, and make yourself easy. I did not suspect, till my last letter was posted, that it might be too strong. I had been counting almost the hours till your arrival for some time. As to coming down again I cannot think of it, for though I could perhaps better spare the time at present from painting than I could at any part of the last month, I find I must now go hard to work to finish my lectures, as the law says they must be delivered the second year after the election.'

The Academy had appointed Opie Professor of Painting in the place of Fuseli, and he was now trying his hand at a new form of composition, and not without well-deserved success. But the strain was too great for this eager mind. Opie painted all day; of an evening he worked at his lectures on painting. From September to February he allowed himself no rest. He was not a man who worked with ease; all he did cost him much effort and struggle. After delivering his first lecture, he complained that he could not sleep. It had been a great success; his colleagues had complimented him, and accompanied him to his house. He was able to complete the course, but immediately afterwards he sickened. No one could discover what was amiss; the languor and fever increased day by day.

His wife nursed him devotedly, and a favourite sister of his came to help her. Afterwards it was of consolation to the widow to remember that no hired nurse had been by his bedside, and that they had been able to do everything for him themselves. One thing troubled him as he lay dying; it was the thought of a picture which he had not been able to complete in time for the exhibition. A friend and former pupil finished it, and brought it to his bedside. He said with a smile, ' Take it away, it will do now.'

To the last he imagined that he was painting upon this picture, and he moved his arms as though he were at work. His illness was inflammation of the brain. He was only forty-five when he died, and he was buried in St. Paul's, and laid by Sir Joshua, his great master.

The portrait of Opie, as it is engraved in Alan Cunningham's Life, is that of a simple, noble-looking man, with a good thoughtful face and a fine head. Northcote, Nollekens, Horne Tooke, all his friends spoke warmly of him. ' A man of powerful understanding and ready apprehension,' says one. ' Mr. Opie crowds more wisdom into a few words than almost anybody I ever saw,' says another. ' I do not say that he was always right,' says Northcote ; ' but he always put your thoughts into a new track that was worth following.' Some two years after his death the lectures which had cost so much were

published, with a memoir by Mrs. Opie. Sir James
Mackintosh has written one of his delightful criticisms
upon the book :—

The cultivation of every science and the practice of every
art are in fact a species of action, and require ardent zeal and
unshaken courage. . . . Originality can hardly exist without
vigour of character. . . . The discoverer or inventor may
indeed be most eminently wanting in decision in the general
concerns of life, but he must possess it in those pursuits in
which he is successful. Opie is a remarkable instance of the
natural union of these superior qualities, both of which he
possesses in a high degree. . . . He is inferior in elegance to
Sir Joshua, but he is superior in strength ; he strikes more,
though he charms less. . . . Opie is by turns an advocate, a
controvertist, a panegyrist, a critic ; Sir Joshua more uniformly
fixes his mind on general and permanent principles, and certainly approaches more nearly to the elevation and tranquillity
which seem to characterise the philosophic teacher of an elegant
art.

## IX.

Mrs. Opie went back, soon after her husband's death,
to Norwich, to her early home, her father's house; nor
was she a widow indeed while she still had this tender
love and protection.

That which strikes one most as one reads the accounts
of Mrs. Opie is the artlessness and perfect simplicity of
her nature. The deepest feeling of her life was her
tender love for her father, and if she remained younger

than most women do, it may have been partly from the great blessing which was hers so long, that of a father's home. Time passed, and by degrees she resumed her old life, and came out and about among her friends. Sorrow does not change a nature, it expresses certain qualities which have been there all along.

So Mrs. Opie came up to London once more, and welcomed and was made welcome by many interesting people. Lord Erskine is her friend always; she visits Madame de Staël; she is constantly in company with Sydney Smith, the ever-welcome as she calls him. Lord Bryon, Sheridan, Lord Dudley, all appear upon her scene. There is a pretty story of her singing her best to Lady Sarah Napier, old, blind, and saddened, but still happy in that she had her sons to guide and to protect her steps. Among her many entertainments, Mrs. Opie amusingly describes a dinner at Sir James Mackintosh's, to which most of the guests had been asked at different hours, varying from six to half-past seven, when Baron William von Humboldt arrives. He writes to her next day, calling her Mademoiselle Opie, ' no doubt from my juvenile appearance,' she adds, writing to her father. It is indeed remarkable to read of her spirits long after middle life, her interest and capacity for amusement. She pays 4*l*. for a ticket to a ball given to the Duke of Wellington; she describes this and many other masquerades and gaieties, and the blue ball, and the pink ball, and the twenty-seven carriages at her door, and her sight of the Emperor of Russia in her hotel. When the rest of the ladies crowd round, eager to touch his clothes, Mrs. Opie, carried away by the general craze, encircles his wrist with her finger and thumb. Apart from these passing fancies, she is in delightful society.

Baron Alderson, her cousin and friend, was always kind and affectionate to her. The pretty little story is well known of his taking her home in her Quaker dress in the Judges' state-coach at Norwich, saying, 'Come, Brother Opie,' as he offered her his arm to lead her to the carriage. She used to stay at his house in London, and almost the last visit she ever paid was to him.

One of the most interesting of her descriptions is that of her meeting with Sir Walter Scott and with Wordsworth at a breakfast in Mount Street, and of Sir Walter's delightful talk and animated stories. One can imagine him laughing and describing a Cockney's terrors in the Highlands, when the whole hunt goes galloping down the crags, as is their North-country fashion. 'The gifted man,' says Mrs. Opie, with her old-fashioned adjectives, 'condescended to speak to me of my "Father and Daughter.' He then went on faithfully to praise his old friend Joanna

Baillie and her tragedies, and to describe a tragedy he
once thought of writing himself. He should have had
no love in it. His hero should have been the uncle
of his heroine, a sort of misanthrope, with only one
affection in his heart, love for his niece, like a solitary
gleam of sunshine lighting the dark tower of some ruined
and lonely dwelling.'

'It might perhaps be a weakness,' says the Friend,
long after recalling this event, 'but I must confess how
greatly I was pleased at the time.' No wonder she was
pleased that the great wizard should have liked her novel.

It would be impossible to attempt a serious critique of
Mrs. Opie's stories. They are artless, graceful, written
with an innocent good faith which disarms criticism.
That Southey, Sydney Smith, and Mackintosh should also
have read them and praised them may, as I have said,
prove as much for the personal charm of the writer, and
her warm sunshine of pleasant companionship, as for the
books themselves. They seem to have run through many
editions, and to have received no little encouragement.
Morality and sensation alternate in her pages. Monsters
abound there. They hire young men to act base parts, to
hold villainous conversations which the husbands are
intended to overhear. They plot and scheme to ruin the
fair fame and domestic happiness of the charming heroines,

but they are justly punished, and their plots are defeated.
One villain, on his way to an appointment with a married
woman, receives so severe a blow upon the head from her
brother, that he dies in agonies of fruitless remorse.
Another, who incautiously boasts aloud his deep-laid
scheme against Constantia's reputation in the dark recesses
of a stage-coach, is unexpectedly seized by the arm. A
stranger in the corner, whom he had not noticed, was no
other than the baronet whom Constantia has loved all
along. The dawn breaks in brightly, shining on the
stranger's face : baffled, disgraced, the wicked schemer
leaves the coach at the very next stage, and Constantia's
happiness is ensured by a brilliant marriage with the man
she loves. ' Lucy is the dark sky,' cries another lovely
heroine, ' but you, my lord, and my smiling children,
these are the rainbow that illumines it; and who would
look at the gloom that see the many tinted Iris ? not I,
indeed.' 'Valentine's Eve,' from which this is quoted,
was published after John Opie's death. So was a novel
called ' Temper,' and the ' Tales of Real Life.' Mrs. Opie,
however, gave up writing novels when she joined the
Society of Friends.

For some years past, Mrs. Opie had been thrown more
and more in the company of a very noble and remarkable
race of men and women living quietly in their beautiful

homes in the neighbourhood of Norwich, but of an influence daily growing—handsome people, prosperous, generous, with a sort of natural Priesthood belonging to them. Scorning to live for themselves alone, the Gurneys were the dispensers and originators of a hundred useful and benevolent enterprises in Norwich and elsewhere. They were Quakers, and merchants, and bankers. How much of their strength lay in their wealth and prosperity, how much in their enthusiasm, their high spirits, voluntarily curbed, their natural instinct both to lead and to protect, it would be idle to discuss. It is always difficult for people who believe in the all-importance of the present to judge of others, whose firm creed is that the present is nothing as compared to the future. Chief among this remarkable family was Elizabeth Gurney, the wife of Josiah Fry, the mother of many children, and the good angel, indeed, of the unhappy captives of those barbarous days, prisoners, to whose utter gloom and misery she brought some rays of hope. There are few figures more striking than that of the noble Quaker lady starting on her generous mission, comforting the children, easing the chains of the captives. No domineering Jellyby, but a motherly, deep-hearted woman ; shy, and yet from her very timidity gaining an influence, which less sensitive natures often fail to win. One likes to imagine the dignified sweet face coming

in—the comforting Friend in the quiet garb of the Quaker
woman standing at the gates of those terrible places, bidding the despairing prisoners be of good hope.

Elizabeth Fry's whole life was a mission of love and
help to others ; her brothers and her many relations
heartily joined and assisted her in many plans and efforts.

For Joseph John Gurney, the head of the Norwich
family, Mrs. Opie is said to have had a feeling amounting
to more than friendship. Be this as it may, it is no wonder
that so warm-hearted and impressionable a woman should
have been influenced by the calm goodness of the friends
with whom she was now thrown. It is evident enough,
nor does she attempt to conceal the fact, that the admiration and interest she feels for John Joseph Gurney are very
deep motive powers. There comes a time in most lives,
especially in the lives of women, when all the habits and
certainties of youth have passed away, when life has to be
built up again upon the foundations indeed of the past, the
friendships, the memories, the habits of early life, but with
new places and things to absorb and to interest, new hearts
to love. And one day people wake up to find that the
friends of their choice have become their home. People
are stranded perhaps seeking their share in life's allowance,
and suddenly they come upon something, with all the
charm which belongs to deliberate choice, as well as that of

natural affinity.  How well one can realise the extraordinary
comfort that Amelia Opie must have found in the kind
friends and neighbours with whom she was now thrown !
Her father was a very old man, dying slowly by inches.
Her own life of struggle, animation, intelligence, was
over, as she imagined, for ever.  No wonder if for a time
she was carried away, if she forgot her own nature, her
own imperative necessities, in sympathy with this new
revelation.  Here was a new existence, here was a Living
Church ready to draw her within its saving walls.  John
Joseph Gurney must have been a man of extraordinary
personal influence.  For a long time past he had been
writing to her seriously.  At last, to the surprise of the
world, though not without long deliberation and her
father's full approval, she joined the Society of Friends,
put on their dress, and adopted their peculiar phraseology.
People were surprised at the time, but I think it would
have been still more surprising if she had not joined them.
J. J. Gurney, in one of his letters, somewhat magnificently
describes Mrs. Opie as offering up her many talents and
accomplishments a brilliant sacrifice to her new-found per-
suasions.  ' Illustrations of Lying,' moral anecdotes on the
borderland of imagination, are all that she is henceforth
allowed.  ' I am bound in a degree not to invent a story,
because when I became a Friend it was required of me not

to do so, she writes to Miss Mitford, who had asked her to contribute to an annual. Miss Mitford's description of Mrs. Opie, ' Quakerised all over, and calling Mr. Haydon ' Friend Benjamin,' is amusing enough ; and so also is the account of the visiting card she had printed after she became a Quaker, with ' Amelia Opie,' without any prefix, as is the Quaker way ; also, as is not their way, with a wreath of embossed pink roses surrounding the name. There is an account of Mrs. Opie published in the ' Edinburgh Review,' in a delightful article entitled the ' Worthies of Norwich,' which brings one almost into her very presence.

Amelia Opie at the end of the last century and Amelia Opie in the garb and with the speech of a member of the Society of Friends sounds like two separate personages, but no one who recollects the gay little songs which at seventy she used to sing with lively gesture, the fragments of drama to which, with the zest of an innate actress, she occasionally treated her young friends, or the elaborate faultlessness of her appearance—the shining folds and long train of her pale satin draperies, the high, transparent cap, the crisp fichu crossed over the breast, which set off to advantage the charming little plump figure with its rounded lines—could fail to recognise the same characteristics which sparkled about the wearer of the pink calico domino in which she frolicked incognito 'till she was tired ' at a ball given by the Duke of Wellington in 1814, or of the eight blue feathers which crowned the waving tresses of her flaxen hair as a bride.

Doctor Alderson died in October 1825, and Mrs. Opie was

left alone. She was very forlorn when her father died.
She had no close ties to carry her on peacefully from middle
age to the end of life. The great break had come ; she was
miserable, and, as mourners do, she falls upon herself and
beats her breast. All through these sad years her friends
at Northrepps and at Earlham were her chief help and
consolation. As time passed her deep sorrow was calmed,
when peaceful memories had succeeded to the keen anguish
of her good old father's loss. She must have suffered
deeply ; she tried hard to be brave, but her courage failed
her at times : she tried hard to do her duty ; and her
kindness and charity were unfailing, for she was herself
still, although so unhappy. Her journals are pathetic in
their humility and self-reproaches for imaginary omissions.
She is lonely ; out of heart, out of hope. 'I am so dissatisfied with myself that I hardly dare ask or expect a
blessing upon my labours,' she says ; and long lists of kind
and fatiguing offices, of visits to sick people and poor people,
to workhouses and prisons, are interspersed with expressions
of self-blame.

The writer can remember as a child speculating as she
watched the straight-cut figure of a Quaker lady standing
in the deep window of an old mansion that overlooked the
Luxembourg Gardens at Paris, with all their perfume and

blooming scent of lilac and sweet echoes of children, while
the quiet figure stood looking down upon it all from—to a
child—such an immeasurable distance. As one grows older
one becomes more used to garbs of different fashions and
cut, and one can believe in present sunlight and the scent
of flowering trees and the happy sound of children's voices
going straight to living hearts beneath their several dis-
guises, and Mrs. Opie, notwithstanding her Quaker dress,
loved bright colours and gay sunlight. She was one of those
who gladly made life happy for others, who naturally turned
to bright and happy things herself. When at last she began
to recover from the blow which had fallen so heavily upon
her she went from Norwich to the Lakes and Fells for re-
freshment, and then to Cornwall, and among its green seas
and softly clothed cliffs she found good friends (as most
people do who go to that kind and hospitable county), and
her husband's relations, who welcomed her kindly. As she
recovered by degrees she began to see something of her old
companions. She went to London to attend the May meet-
ings of the Society, and I heard an anecdote not long ago
which must have occurred on some one of these later visits
there.

One day when some people were sitting at breakfast at
Samuel Rogers's, and talking as people do who belong to
the agreeable classes, the conversation happened to turn

upon the affection of a father for his only child, when an elderly lady who had been sitting at the table, and who was remarkable for her Quaker dress, her frills and spotless folds, her calm and striking appearance, started up suddenly, burst into a passion of tears, and had to be led sobbing out of the room. She did not return, and the lady who remembers the incident, herself a young bride at the time, told me it made all the more impression upon her at the time because she was told that the Quaker lady was Mrs. Opie. My friend was just beginning her life. Mrs. Opie must have been ending hers. It is not often that women, when youth is long past, shed sudden and passionate tears of mere emotion, nor perhaps would a Quaker, trained from early childhood to calm moods and calm expressions, have been so suddenly overpoweringly affected; but Mrs. Opie was no born daughter of the community, she was excitable and impulsive to the last. I have heard a lady who knew her well describe her, late in life, laughing heartily and impetuously thrusting a somewhat starched-up Friend into a deep arm-chair exclaiming, 'I will hurl thee into the bottomless pit.'

### X.

> At sight of thee, O Tricolor,
> I seem to feel youth's hours return,
> The loved, the lost !

So writes Mrs. Opie at the age of sixty, reviving, delighting, as she catches sight of her beloved Paris once more, and breathes its clear and life-giving air, and looks out across its gardens and glittering gables and spires, and again meets her French acquaintances, and throws herself into their arms and into their interests with all her old warmth and excitability. The little grey bonnet only gives certain incongruous piquancy to her pleasant, kind-hearted exuberance. She returns to England, but far-away echoes reach her soon of changes and revolutions concerning all the people for whom her regard is so warm. In August, 1830, came the news of a new revolution—'The Chamber of Deputies dissolved for ever; the liberty of the press abolished; king, ministers, court, and ambassadors flying from Paris to Vincennes; cannon planted against the city; 5,000 people killed, and the Rue de Rivoli running with blood.' No wonder such rumours stirred and overwhelmed the staunch but excitable lady. 'You will readily believe how anxious, interested, and excited I feel,' she says; and then she goes on to speak of Lafayette, 'miraculously preserved through two revolutions, and in chains and in a dungeon, now the leading mind in another conflict, and lifting not only an armed but a restraining hand in a third revolution.'

Her heart was with her French friends and intimates, and though she kept silence she was not the less determined to follow its leading, and, without announcing her

intention, she started off from Norwich and, after travelling without intermission, once more arrived in her
beloved city.  But what was become of the Revolution ?
'Paris seemed as bright and peaceful as I had seen it
thirteen months ago !  The people, the busy people
passing to and fro, and soldiers, omnibuses, cabriolets,
citadenes, carts, horsemen hurrying along the Rue de
Rivoli, while foot passengers were crossing the gardens, or
loungers were sitting on its benches to enjoy the beauty
of the May-November.'  She describes two men crossing
the Place Royale singing a national song, the result of the
Revolution :—

> Pour briser leurs masses profondes,
> Qui conduit nos drapeaux sanglants,
> C'est la Liberté de deux mondes,
> C'est Lafayette en cheveux blancs.

Mrs. Opie was full of enthusiasm for noble Lafayette
surveying his court of turbulent intrigue and shifting
politics ; for Cuvier in his own realm, among more
tranquil laws, less mutable decrees.  She should have
been born a Frenchwoman, to play a real and brilliant
part among all these scenes and people, instead of only
looking on.  Something stirred in her veins too eager and
bubbling for an Englishwoman's scant share of life and
outward events.  No wonder that her friends at Norwich

were anxious, and urged her to return. They heard of her living in the midst of excitement, of admiration, and with persons of a different religion and way of thinking to themselves. Their warning admonitions carried their weight; that little Quaker bonnet which she took so much care of was a talisman, drawing the most friendly of Friends away from the place of her adoption. But she came back unchanged to her home, to her quiet associations; she had lost none of her spirits, none of her cheerful interest in her natural surroundings. As life burnt on her kind soul seemed to shine more and more brightly. Every one came to see her, to be cheered and warmed by her genial spirit. She loved flowers, of which her room was full. She had a sort of passion for prisms, says her biographer; she had several set in a frame and mounted like a screen, and the colour flew about the little room. She kept up a great correspondence; she was never tired of writing, though the letters on other people's business were apt to prove a serious burden at times. But she lives on only to be of use. 'Take care of indulging in little selfishnesses,' she writes in her diary; 'learn to consider others in trifles: the mind so disciplined will find it easier to fulfil the greater duties, and the character will not exhibit that trying inconsistency which one sees in great and often in pious persons.' Her health fails, but not her courage. She goes up to London for the last time to her cousin's house. She is interested in all the people she meets, in their wants and necessities, in the events of the time. She returns home, contented with all; with the house which she feels so 'desirable to die in,' with her window through which she can view the woods and rising ground of Thorpe. ' My prisms to-day are quite in their glory,' she writes; ' the atmosphere must be very clear, for the radiance is brighter than ever I saw it before ; ' and then she wonders whether the mansions in heaven will be draped in such brightness ; and so to the last the gentle, bright, *rainbow* lady remained surrounded by kind and smiling faces, by pictures, by flowers, and with the light of her favourite prismatic colours shining round about the couch on which she lay.

# JANE AUSTEN.

## 1775—1817.

‘A mesure qu’on a plus d’esprit on trouve qu’il y a plus d’hommes originaux. Les gens du commun ne trouvent pas de différence entre les hommes.’—PASCAL.

‘I DID not know that you were a studier of character,’ says Bingley to Elizabeth. ‘It must be an amusing study.’

‘Yes, but intricate characters are the most amusing. They have at least that advantage.’

‘The country,’ said Darcy, ‘can in general supply but few subjects for such a study. In a country neighbourhood you move in a very confined and unvarying society.’

‘But people themselves alter so much,’ Elizabeth answers, ‘that there is something new to be observed in them for ever.’

‘Yes, indeed,’ cried Mrs. Bennet, offended by Darcy’s manner of mentioning a country neighbourhood; ‘I assure you that we have quite as much of *that* going on in the country as in town.’

‘Everybody was surprised, and Darcy, after looking at her for a moment, turned silently away. Mrs. Bennet, who

fancied she had gained a complete victory over him, continued her triumph.'

These people belong to a whole world of familiar
acquaintances, who are, notwithstanding their old-fashioned dresses and quaint expressions, more alive to us than
a great many of the people among whom we live. We
know so much more about them to begin with. Notwithstanding a certain reticence and self-control which seems
to belong to their age, and with all their quaint dresses,
and ceremonies, and manners, the ladies and gentlemen in
' Pride and Prejudice ' and its companion novels seem like
living people out of our own acquaintance transported
bodily into a bygone age, represented in the half-dozen
books that contain Jane Austen's works. Dear books !
bright, sparkling with wit and animation, in which the
homely heroines charm, the dull hours fly, and the very
bores are enchanting.

Could we but study our own bores as Miss Austen must
have studied hers in her country village, what a delightful
world this might be !—a world of Norris's economical great
walkers, with dining-room tables to dispose of ; of Lady
Bertrams on sofas, with their placid ' Do not act anything
improper, my dears ; Sir Thomas would not like it ; ' of
Bennets, Goddards, Bates's ; of Mr. Collins's ; of Rush-
brooks, with two-and-forty speeches apiece—a world of

Mrs. Eltons. . . . .Inimitable woman! she must be alive at this very moment, if we but knew where to find her, her basket on her arm, her nods and all-importance, with Maple Grove and the Sucklings in the background. She would be much excited were she aware how she is esteemed by a late Chancellor of the Exchequer, who is well acquainted with Maple Grove and Selina too. It might console her for Mr. Knightly's shabby marriage.

All these people nearly start out of the pages, so natural and unaffected are they, and yet they never lived except in the imagination of one lady with bright eyes, who sat down some seventy years ago to an old mahogany desk in a quiet country parlour, and evoked them for us. One seems to see the picture of the unknown friend who has charmed us so long—charmed away dull hours, created neighbours and companions for us in lonely places, conferring happiness and harmless mirth upon generations to come. One can picture her as she sits erect, with her long and graceful figure, her full round face, her bright eyes cast down,—Jane Austen, ' the woman of whom England is justly proud '—whose method generous Macaulay has placed near Shakespeare. She is writing in secret, putting away her work when visitors come in, unconscious, modest, hidden at home in heart, as she was in her sweet and womanly life, with the wisdom of the serpent indeed and the harmlessness of a dove.

Some one said just now that many people seem to be so proud of seeing a joke at all, that they impress it upon you until you are perfectly wearied by it. Jane Austen was not of these; her humour flows gentle and spontaneous; it is no elaborate mechanism nor artificial fountain, but a bright natural stream, rippling and trickling over every stone and sparkling in the sunshine. We should be surprised now-a-days to hear a young lady announce herself as a studier of character. From her quiet home in the country lane this one reads to us a real page from the absorbing pathetic humorous book of human nature—a book that we can most of us understand when it is translated into plain English; but of which the quaint and illegible characters are often difficult to decipher for ourselves. It is a study which, with all respect for Darcy's opinion, must require something of country-like calm and concentration and freedom of mind. It is difficult, for instance, for a too impulsive student not to attribute something of his own moods to his specimens instead of dispassionately contemplating them from a critical distance.

Besides the natural fun and wit and life of her characters, 'all perfectly discriminated,' as Macaulay says, Jane Austen has the gift of telling a story in a way that has never been surpassed. She rules her places, times, characters, and marshals them with unerring precision. In her special gift for organisation she seems almost unequalled. Her picnics are models for all future and past picnics; her combinations of feelings, of conversation, of gentlemen and ladies, are so natural and lifelike that reading to criticise is impossible to some of us—the scene carries us away, and we forget to look for the art by which it is recorded. Her machinery is simple but complete; events group themselves so vividly and naturally in her mind that, in describing imaginary scenes, we seem not only to read them, but to live them, to see the people coming and going: the gentlemen courteous and in top-boots, the ladies demure and piquant; we can almost hear them talking to one another. No retrospects; no abrupt flights; as in real life days and events follow one another. Last Tuesday does not suddenly start into existence all out of place; nor does 1790 appear upon the scene when we are well on in '21. Countries and continents do not fly from hero to hero, nor do long and divergent adventures happen to unimportant members of the company. With Jane Austen days, hours, minutes succeed each other like clock-work, one central figure is always present on the scene, that figure is always prepared for company. Miss Edwards's curl-papers are almost the only approach to dishabille in

her stories. There are postchaises in readiness to convey
the characters from Bath or Lyme to Uppercross, to
Fullerton, from Gracechurch Street to Meryton, as their
business takes them. Mr. Knightly rides from Brunswick
Square to Hartfield, by a road that Miss Austen herself
must have travelled in the curricle with her brother, driving
to London on a summer's day. It was a wet ride for Mr.
Knightly, followed by that never-to-be-forgotten afternoon in the shrubbery, when the wind had changed into a
softer quarter, the clouds were carried off, and Emma,
walking in the sunshine, with spirits freshened and
thoughts a little relieved, and thinking of Mr. Knightly
as sixteen miles away, meets him at the garden door ; and
everybody, I think, must be the happier, for the happiness
and certainty that one half-hour gave to Emma and her
' indifferent ' lover.

There is a little extract from one of Miss Austen's
letters to a niece, which shows that all this successful
organisation was not brought about by chance alone, but
came from careful workmanship.

' Your aunt C.,' she says, ' does not like desultory
novels, and is rather fearful that yours will be too much
so—that there will be too frequent a change from one set
of people to another, and that circumstances will be sometimes introduced of apparent consequence, which will lead

to nothing. It will not be so great an objection to me. I allow much more latitude than she does, and think nature and spirit cover many sins of a wandering story. . . .'

But, though the sins of a wandering story may be covered, the virtues of a well-told one make themselves felt unconsciously, and without an effort. Some books and people are delightful, we can scarce tell why; they are not so clever as others that weary and fatigue us. It is a certain effort to read a story, however touching, that is disconnected and badly related. It is like an ill-drawn picture, of which the colouring is good. Jane Austen possessed both gifts of colour and of drawing. She could see human nature as it was; with near-sighted eyes, it is true; but having seen, she could combine her picture by her art, and colour it from life. How delightful the people are who play at cards, and pay their addresses to one another, and sup, and discuss each other's affairs! Take Mr. Bennet's reception of his sons-in-law. Take Sir Walter Elliot compassionating the navy and Admiral Baldwin—'nine grey hairs of a side, and nothing but a dab of powder at top—a wretched example of what a sea-faring life can do, for men who are exposed to every climate and weather until they are not fit to be seen. It is a pity they are not knocked on the head at once, before they reach Admiral Baldwin's age. . . .' Or shall we quote the scene of Fanny Price's return when she comes to visit her family at Portsmouth ; in all daughterly agitation and excitement, and the brother's and father's and sister's reception of her. . . . 'A stare or two at Fanny was all the voluntary notice that her brother bestowed, but he made no objection to her kissing him, though still entirely engaged in detailing further particulars of the " Thrush's " going out of harbour, in which he had a strong right of interest, being about to commence his career of seamanship in her at this very time. After the mother and daughter have received her, Fanny's seafaring father comes in, and does not notice her at first in his excitement. " Captain Walsh thinks you will certainly have a cruise to the westward with the ' Elephant ' by —— I wish you may. But old Scholey was saying just now that he thought you would be sent first to the ' Texel.' Well, well, we are ready whatever happens. But by —— you lost a fine sight by not being here in the morning to see the ' Thrush ' go out of harbour. I would not have been out of the way for a thousand pounds. Old Scholey ran in at breakfast time to say she had slipped her moorings and was coming out. I jumped up and made but two steps to the platform. If ever there was a perfect beauty afloat she is one ; and there she lies at Spithead, and anybody in England would take her for an eight-and-twenty. I was upon the platform for two hours this afternoon looking at her. She lies close to the 'Endymion,' between her and the 'Cleopatra,' just to the eastward of the sheer hulk." '

' " Ha !" cried William, " *that's* just where I should have put her myself. It's the best berth in Spithead. But here is my sister, sir ; here is Fanny, turning and leading her forward—it is so dark you do not see her." '

' With an acknowledgment that he had quite forgot her, Mr. Price now received his daughter, and having given her a cordial hug and observed that she was grown into a woman and he supposed would be wanting a husband soon, seemed very much inclined to forget her again.'

How admirably it is all told ! how we hear them all talking !

From her own brothers Jane Austen learned her accurate knowledge of ships and seafaring things, from her own observation she must have gathered her delightful droll science of men and women and their ways and various destinations. Who will not recognise Mrs. Norris in that master-touch by which she removes the curtain to save Sir Thomas's feelings, that curtain which had been prepared for the private theatricals he so greatly disapproved of ? Mrs. Norris thoughtfully carries it off to her cottage, where she happened to be particularly in want of green baize.

## II.

The charm of friends of pen-and-ink is their un-
changeableness. We go to them when we want them. We
know where to seek them; we know what to expect from
them.    They are never preoccupied; they are always
' at home;' they never turn their backs nor walk away as
people do in real life, nor let their houses and leave the
neighbourhood, and disappear for weeks together; they
are never taken up with strange people, nor suddenly
absorbed into some more genteel society, or by some
nearer fancy.    Even the most volatile among them is to
be counted upon.    We may have neglected them, and yet
when we meet again there are the familiar old friends,
and we seem to find our own old selves again in their
company.    For us time has, perhaps, passed away; feelings
have swept by, leaving interests and recollections in their
place; but at all ages there must be days that belong to
our youth, hours that will recur so long as men forbear
and women remember, and life itself exists.    Perhaps the
most fashionable marriage on the *tapis* no longer excites
us very much, but the sentiment of an Emma or an Anne
Elliot comes home to some of us as vividly as ever.    It is
something to have such old friends who are so young.    An

Emma, blooming, without a wrinkle or a grey hair, after twenty years' acquaintance ; an Elizabeth Bennet, sprightly and charming ever. . . .

In the ' Roundabout Papers ' there is a passage about the pen-and-ink friends my father loved :—

' They used to call the good Sir Walter the " Wizard of the North." What if some writer should appear who can write so *enchantingly* that he shall be able to call into actual life the people whom he invents ?  What if Mignon, and Margaret, and Goetz vòn Berlichingen are alive now (though I don't say they are visible), and Dugald Dalgetty and Ivanhoe were to step in at that open window by the little garden yonder ?  Suppose Uncas and our noble old Leather Stocking were to glide in silent ?  Suppose Athos, Porthos, and Aramis should enter, with a noiseless swagger, curling their moustaches ?  And dearest Amelia Booth, on Uncle Toby's arm ; and Tittlebat Titmouse with his hair dyed green ; and all the Crummles company of comedians, with the Gil Blas troop ; and Sir Roger de Coverley ; and the greatest of all crazy gentlemen, the Knight of La Mancha, with his blessed squire ?  I say to you, I look rather wistfully towards the window, musing upon these people.  Were any of them to enter, I think I should not be very much frightened. . . .'

Are not such friends as these, and others unnamed here,

but who will come unannounced to join the goodly company, creations that, like some people, do actually make part of our existence, and make us the better for theirs? To express some vague feelings is to stamp them. Have we any one of us a friend in a Knight of La Mancha, a Colonel Newcome, a Sir Roger de Coverley? They live for us even though they may have never lived. They are, and do actually make part of our lives, one of the best and noblest parts. To love them is like a direct communication with the great and generous minds that conceived them.

It is difficult, reading the novels of succeeding generations, to determine how much each book reflects of the time in which it was written; how much of its character depends upon the mind and the mood of the writer. The greatest minds, the most original, have the least stamp of the age, the most of that dominant natural reality which belongs to all great minds. We know how a landscape changes as the day goes on, and how the scene brightens and gains in beauty as the shadows begin to lengthen. The clearest eyes must see by the light of their own hour. Jane Austen's literary hour must have been a midday hour: bright, unsuggestive, with objects standing clear, without much shadow or elaborate artistic effect. Our own age is more essentially an age of strained emotion, little remains to us of starch, or powder, or courtly reserve. What we have lost in calm, in happiness, in tranquillity, we have gained in emphasis. Our danger is now, not of expressing and feeling too little, but of expressing more than we feel.

The living writers of to-day lead us into distant realms and worlds undreamt of in the placid and easily contented gigot age. Our characters travel by rail and are no longer confined to postchaises. There is certainly a wide difference between Miss Austen's heroines and, let us say, a Maggie Tulliver. One would be curious to know whether, between the human beings who read Jane Austen's books to-day and those who read them fifty years ago, there is as great a contrast. One reason may be, perhaps, that characters in novels are certainly more intimate with us and on less ceremonious terms than in Jane Austen's days, when heroines never gave up a certain gentle self-respect and humour and hardness of heart in which some modern types are a little wanting. Whatever happens they could for the most part speak of quietly and without bitterness. Love with them does not mean a passion so much as an interest, deep, silent, not quite incompatible with a secondary flirtation. Marianne Dashwood's tears are evidently meant to be dried. Jane Bennet smiles, sighs

P

and makes excuses for Bingley's neglect. Emma passes one disagreeable morning making up her mind to the unnatural alliance between Mr. Knightly and Harriet Smith. It was the spirit of the age, and, perhaps, one not to be unenvied. It was not that Jane Austen herself was incapable of understanding a deeper feeling. In the last written page of her last written book, there is an expression of the deepest and truest experience. Annie Elliot's talk with Captain Benfield is the touching utterance of a good woman's feelings. They are speaking of men and of women's affections. ' You are always labouring and toiling,' she says, ' exposed to every risk and hardship. Your home, country, friends, all united ; neither time nor life to be called your own. It would be too hard, indeed (with a faltering voice), if a woman's feelings were to be added to all this.'

Further on she says, eagerly : ' I hope I do justice to all that is felt by you, and by those who resemble you. God forbid that I should undervalue the warm and faithful feelings of any of my fellow-creatures. I should deserve utter contempt if I dared to suppose that true attachment and constancy were known only by woman. No ! I believe you capable of everything good and great in your married lives. I believe you equal to every important exertion, and to every domestic forbearance so long as—if I may be allowed the expression—so long as you have an object; I mean while the woman you love lives and lives for you. *All the privilege I claim for my own sex (it is not a very enviable one, you need not court it) is that of loving longest when existence or when hope is gone.'*

She could not immediately have uttered another sentence—her heart was too full, her breath too much oppressed.

Dear Anne Elliot !—sweet, impulsive, womanly, tender-hearted—one can almost hear her voice, pleading the cause of all true women. In those days when, perhaps, people's nerves were stronger than they are now, sentiment may have existed in a less degree, or have been more ruled by judgment, it may have been calmer and more matter-of-fact; and yet Jane Austen, at the very end of her life, wrote thus. Her words seem to ring in our ears after they have been spoken. Anne Elliot must have been Jane Austen herself, speaking for the last time. There is something so true, so womanly about her, that it is impossible not to love her most of all. She is the bright-eyed heroine of the earlier novels, matured, softened, cultivated, to whom fidelity has brought only greater depth and sweetness instead of bitterness and pain.

What a difficult thing it would be to sit down and try to

enumerate the different influences by which our lives have
been affected—influences of other lives, of art, of nature, of
place and circumstance,—of beautiful sights passing before.
our eyes, or painful ones : seasons following in their
course—hills rising on our horizons—scenes of ruin and
desolation—crowded thoroughfares—sounds in our ears,.
jarring or harmonious—the voices of friends, calling,
warning, encouraging—of preachers preaching—of people
in the street below, complaining, and asking our pity!
What long processions of human beings are passing before
us! What trains of thought go sweeping through our
brains! Man seems a strange and ill-kept record of many
and bewildering experiences. Looking at oneself—not as
oneself, but as an abstract human being—one is lost in
wonder at the vast complexities which have been brought
to bear upon it ; lost in wonder, and in disappointment
perhaps, at the discordant result of so great a harmony.
Only we know that the whole diapason is beyond our
grasp : one man cannot hear the note of the grasshoppers,
another is deaf when the cannon sounds. Waiting among
these many echoes and mysteries of every kind, and light
and darkness, and life and death, we seize a note or two of
the great symphony, and try to sing ; and because these
notes happen to jar, we think all is discordant hopeless-
ness. Then come pressing onward in the crowd of life,

voices with some of the notes that are wanting to our own part—voices tuned to the same key as our own, or to an accordant one; making harmony for us as they pass us by. Perhaps this is in life the happiest of all experience, and to few of us there exists any more complete ideal.

And so now and then in our lives, when we learn to love a sweet and noble character, we all feel happier and better for the goodness and charity which is not ours, and yet which seems to belong to us while we are near it. Just as some people and states of mind affect us uncomfortably, so we seem to be true to ourselves with a truthful person, generous-minded with a generous nature; life seems less disappointing and self-seeking when we think of the just and sweet and unselfish spirits, moving untroubled among dinning and distracting influences. These are our friends in the best and noblest sense. We are the happier for their existence,—it is so much gain to us. They may have lived at some distant time, we may never have met face to face, or we may have known them and been blessed by their love ; but their light shines from afar, their life is for us and with us in its generous example ; their song is for our ears, and we hear it and love it still, though the singer may be lying dead.

## III.

A little book, written by one of Jane Austen's nephews, tells with a touching directness and simplicity the story of this good and gifted woman, whose name has long been a household word among us, but of whose history nothing was known until this little volume appeared. It is but the story of a country lady, of quiet days following quiet days of seasons in their course of common events; and yet the history is deeply interesting to those who loved the writer of whom it is written; and as we turn from the story of Jane Austen's life to her books again, we feel more than ever that she, too, was one of those true friends who belong to us inalienably—simple, wise, contented, living in others, one of those whom we seem to have a right to love. Such people belong to all humankind by the very right of their wide and generous sympathies, of their gentle wisdom and loveableness. Jane Austen's life, as it is told by Mr. Austen Legh, is very touching, sweet, and peaceful. It is a country landscape, where the cattle are grazing, the boughs of the great elmtree rocking in the wind: sometimes, as we read, they come falling with a crash into the sweep; birds are flying about the old house, homely in its simple rule. The rafters cross the whitewashed ceilings, the beams project into the room below. We can see it all: the parlour with the horsehair sofa, the scant, quaint furniture, the old-fashioned garden outside, with its flowers and vegetables combined, and along the south side of the garden the green terrace sloping away.

There is a pretty description of the sisters' devotion to one another (when Cassandra went to school little Jane accompanied her, the sisters could not be parted), of the family party, of the old place, ' where there are hedge-rows winding, with green shady footpaths within the copse ; where the earliest primroses and hyacinths are found.' There is the wood-walk, with its rustic seats, leading to the meadows ; the church-walk leading to the church, ' which is far from the hum of the village, and within sight of no habitation, except a glimpse of the grey manor-house through its circling screen of sycamores. Sweet violets, both purple and white, grow in abundance beneath its south wall. Large elms protrude their rough branches, old hawthorns shed their blossoms over the graves, and the hollow yew-tree must be at least coëval with the church.'

One may read the account of Catherine Morland's home with new interest, from the hint which is given of its likeness to the old house at Steventon, where dwelt the unknown friend whose voice we seem to hear at last, and whose face we seem to recognise, her bright eyes and brown curly hair, her quick and graceful figure. One can picture the children who are playing at the door of the old parsonage, and calling for Aunt Jane. One can imagine her pretty ways with them, her sympathy for the active, their games and imaginations. There is Cassandra. She is older than her sister, more critical, more beautiful, more reserved. There is the mother of the family, with her keen wit and clear mind ; the handsome father—' the handsome proctor,' as he was called; the five brothers, driving up the lane. Tranquil summer passes by, the winter days go by ; the young lady still sits writing at the old mahogany desk, and smiling, perhaps, at her own fancies, and hiding them away with her papers at the sound of coming steps. Now, the modest papers, printed and reprinted, lie in every hand, the fancies disport themselves at their will in the wisest brains and the most foolish.

It must have been at Steventon—Jane Austen's earliest home—that Mr. Collins first made his appearance (Lady Catherine not objecting, as we know, to his occasional absence on a Sunday, provided another clergyman was engaged to do the duty of the day), and here, conversing with Miss Jane, that he must have made many of his profoundest observations upon human nature; remarking, among other things, that resignation is never so perfect as when the blessing denied begins to lose somewhat of its value in our estimation, and propounding his celebrated theory about the usual practice of elegant females. It must have been here, too, that poor Mrs. Bennet declared, with some justice, that once estates are entailed, one can never tell how they will go; here, too, that Mrs. Allen's sprigged muslin and John Thorpe's rodomontades were woven; that his gig was built, ' curricle-hung lamps, seat, trunk, sword-case, splashboard, silver moulding, all, you see, complete. The ironwork as good as new, or better. He asked fifty guineas. . . . . I closed with him directly, threw down the money, and the carriage was mine.'

' And I am sure,' said Catherine, ' I know so little of such things, that I cannot judge whether it was cheap or dear.'

' Neither the one nor the other,' says John Thorpe.

Mrs. Palmer was also born at Steventon—that good-humoured lady in ' Sense and Sensibility,' who thinks it so ridiculous that her husband never hears her when she speaks to him. We are told that Marianne and Ellinor have been supposed to represent Cassandra and Jane Austen; but Mr. Austen Legh says that he can trace no resemblance. Jane Austen is not twenty when this book is written, and only twenty-one when 'Pride and Preju-dice' is first devised.

Cousins presently come on the scene, and amongst them the romantic figure of a young, widowed Comtesse de Feuillade, flying from the Revolution to her uncle's home. She is described as a clever and accomplished woman, interested in her young cousins, teaching them French (both Jane and Cassandra knew French), helping in their various schemes, in their theatricals in the barn. She eventually marries her cousin, Henry Austen. The simple family annals are not without their romance; but there is a cruel one for poor Cassandra, whose lover dies abroad, and his death saddens the whole family-party. Jane, too, 'receives the addresses' (do such things as addresses exist nowadays?) 'of a gentleman possessed of good cha-racter and fortune, and of everything, in short, except the subtle power of touching her heart.' One cannot help wondering whether this was a Henry Crawford or an Elton or a Mr. Elliot, or had Jane already seen the person that even Cassandra thought good enough for her sister?

Here, too, is another sorrowful story. The sisters' fate (there is a sad coincidence and similarity in it) was to be undivided; their life, their experience was the same. Some one without a name takes leave of Jane one day, promising

to come back. He never comes back : long afterwards
they hear of his death. The story seems even sadder than
Cassandra's in its silence and uncertainty, for silence and
uncertainty are death in life to some people. . . . .

There is little trace of such a tragedy in Jane Austen's
books—not one morbid word is to be found, not one vain
regret. Hers was not a nature to fall crushed by the
overthrow of one phase of her manifold life. She seems
to have had a natural genius for life, if I may so speak ;
too vivid and genuinely unselfish to fail her in her need.
She could gather every flower, every brightness along her
road. Good spirit, content, all the interests of a happy
and observant nature were hers. Her gentle humour and
wit and interest cannot have failed.

It is impossible to calculate the difference of the grasp
by which one or another human being realises existence
and the things relating to it, nor how much more vivid life
seems to some than to others. Jane Austen, while her
existence lasted, realised it, and made the best use of the
gifts that were hers. Yet, when her life was ending, then
it was given to her to understand the change that was at
hand ; as willingly as she had lived, she died. Some
people seem scarcely to rise up to their own work, to their
own ideal. Jane Austen's life, as it is told by her nephew,
is beyond her work, which only contained one phase of

that sweet and wise nature—the creative, observant, outward phase. For her home, for her sister, for her friends, she kept the depth and tenderness of her bright and gentle sympathy. She is described as busy with her neat and clever fingers sewing for the poor, working fanciful keepsakes for her friends. There is the cup and ball that she never failed to catch; the spillikens lie in an even ring where she had thrown them; there are her letters, straightly and neatly folded, and fitting smoothly in their creases. There is something sweet, orderly, and consistent in her character and all her tastes—in her fondness for Crabbe and Cowper, in her little joke that she ought to be a Mrs. Crabbe. She sings of an evening old ballads to old-fashioned tunes with a low sweet voice.

Further on we have a glimpse of Jane and her sister in their mobcaps, young still, but dressed soberly beyond their years. One can imagine 'Aunt Jane,' with her brother's children round her knee, telling her delightful stories or listening to theirs, with never-failing sympathy. One can fancy Cassandra, who does not like desultory novels, more prudent and more reserved, and somewhat less of a playfellow, looking down upon the group with elder sister's eyes.

Here is an extract from a letter written at Steventon in 1800 :—

' I have two messages : let me get rid of them, and then my paper will be my own. Mary fully intended writing by Mr. Charles's frank, and only happened entirely to forget it, but will write soon ; and my father wishes Edward to send him a memorandum of the price of hops.

' *Sunday Evening.*

' We have had a dreadful storm of wind in the fore-part of the day, which has done a great deal of mischief among our trees. I was sitting alone in the drawing-room when an odd kind of crash startled me. In a moment afterwards it was repeated. I then went to the window. I reached it just in time to see the last of our two highly valued elms descend into the sweep ! ! !

' The other, which had fallen, I suppose, in the first crash, and which was nearest to the pond, taking a more easterly direction, sank among our screen of chestnuts and firs, knocking down one spruce-fir, breaking off the head of another, and stripping the two corner chestnuts of several branches in its fall. This is not all : the maple bearing the weathercock was broken in two, and what I regret more than all the rest is, that all the three elms that grew in Hall's Meadow, and gave such ornament to it, are gone.'

A certain Mrs. Stent comes into one of these letters ' ejaculating some wonder about the cocks and hens. Mrs.

Stent seems to have tried their patience, and will be known henceforward as having bored Jane Austen.

They leave Steventon when Jane is about twenty-five years of age and go to Bath, from whence a couple of pleasant letters are given us. Jane is writing to her sister. She has visited Miss A., who, like all other young ladies, is considerably genteeler than her parents. She is heartily glad that Cassandra speaks so comfortably of her health and looks : could travelling fifty miles produce such an immediate change ? 'You were looking poorly when you were here, and everybody seemed sensible of it.' Is there any charm in a hack postchaise ? But if there were, Mrs. Craven's carriage might have undone it all. Then Mrs. Stent appears again. 'Poor Mrs. Stent, it has been her lot to be always in the way ; but we must be merciful, for perhaps in time we may come to be Mrs. Stents ourselves, unequal to anything and unwelcome to everybody.' Elsewhere she writes, upon Mrs. ——'s mentioning that she had sent the 'Rejected Addresses' to Mr. H., 'I began talking to her a little about them, and expressed my hope of their having amused her. Her answer was, " Oh dear, yes, very much ; very droll indeed ; the opening of the house and the striking up of the fiddles ! " What she meant, poor woman, who shall say ? '

But there is no malice in Jane Austen. Hers is the

charity of all clear minds, it is only the muddled who are intolerant. All who love Emma and Mr. Knightly must remember the touching little scene in which he reproves her for her thoughtless impatience of poor Miss Bates's volubility.

' You, whom she had known from an infant, whom she had seen grow up from a period when her notice was an honour, to have you now, in thoughtless spirits and in the pride of the moment, laugh at her, humble her. . . . This is not pleasant to you, Emma, and it is very far from pleasant to me, but I must, I will, I will tell you truths while I am satisfied with proving myself your friend by very faithful counsel, and trusting that you will some time or other do me greater justice than you can do me now.'

' While they talked they were advancing towards the carriage : it was ready, and before she could speak again he had handed her in. He had misinterpreted the feeling which kept her face averted and her tongue motionless.' Mr. Knightly's little sermon, in its old-fashioned English, is as applicable now as it was when it was spoken. We know that he was an especial favourite with Jane Austen.

## IV.

Mr. Austen died at Bath, and his family removed to Southampton. In 1811, Mrs. Austen, her daughters, and her niece, settled finally at Chawton, a house belonging to Jane's brother, Mr. Knight (he was adopted by an uncle, whose name he took), and from Chawton all her literary work was given to the world. ' Sense and Sensibility,' ' Pride and Prejudice,' were already written ; but in the next five years, from thirty-five to forty, she set to work seriously, and wrote ' Mansfield Park,' ' Emma,' and ' Persuasion.' Any one who has written a book will know what an amount of labour this represents. . . . One can picture to oneself the little family scene which Jane describes to Cassandra. ' Pride and Prejudice ' just come down in a parcel from town ; the unsuspicious Miss B. to dinner ; and Jane and her mother setting to in the evening and reading aloud half the first volume of a new novel sent down by the brother. Unsuspicious Miss B. is delighted. Jane complains of her mother's too rapid way of getting on ; ' though she perfectly understands the characters herself, she cannot speak as they ought. Upon the whole, however,' she says, ' I am quite vain enough and well-satisfied enough.' This is her own criticism of ' Pride and Pre-

judice ':—'The work is rather too light, and bright, and
sparkling. It wants shade. It wants to be stretched out
here and there with a long chapter of sense, if it could be
had ; if not, of solemn specious nonsense about something
unconnected with the story—an essay on writing, a critique
on Walter Scott or the 'History of Bonaparte.'

And so Jane Austen lives quietly working at her labour
of love, interested in her ' own darling children's ' success ;
' the light of the home,' one of the real living children
says afterwards, speaking in the days when she was no
longer there. She goes to London once or twice. Once
she lives for some months in Hans Place, nursing a brother
through an illness. Here it was that she received some
little compliments and messages from the Prince Regent,
to whom she dedicated ' Emma.' He thanks her and ac-
knowledges the handsome volumes, and she laughs and
tells her publisher that at all events his share of the
offering is appreciated, whatever hers may be! We are
also favoured with some valuable suggestions from Mr.
Clarke, the Royal librarian, respecting a very remarkable
clergyman. He is anxious that Miss Austen should de-
lineate one who ' should pass his time between the metro-
polis and the country, something like Beattie's minstrel,
entirely engaged in literature, and no man's enemy but
his own.' Failing to impress this character upon the

authoress, he makes a fresh suggestion, and proposes that she should write a romance illustrative of the august house of Coburg. ' It would be interesting,' he says, ' and very properly dedicated to Prince Leopold.'

To which the authoress replies: 'I could no more write a romance than an epic poem. I could not seriously sit down to write a romance under any other motive than to save my life; and if it were indispensable for me to keep it up, and never relax into laughing at myself or other people, I am sure I should be hung before the first chapter.'

There is a delightful collection of friends suggestions which she has put together, but which is too long to be quoted here. She calls it, ' Plan of a Novel, as suggested by various Friends.'

All this time, while her fame is slowly growing, life passes in the same way as in the old cottage at Chawton. Aunt Jane, with her young face and her mob-cap, makes play-houses for the children, helps them to dress up, invents imaginary conversations for them, supposing that they are all grown up, the day after a ball. One can imagine how delightful a game that must have seemed to the little girls. She built her nest, did this good woman, happily weaving it out of shreds, and ends, and scraps of daily duty, patiently put together; and it was from this nest that she sang the song, bright and brilliant, with quaint thrills and unexpected cadences, that reaches us even here through near a century. The lesson her life seems to teach us is this : Don't let us despise our nests— life is as much made of minutes as of years; let us complete the daily duties; let us patiently gather the twigs and the little scraps of moss, of dried grass together, and see the result!—a whole, completed and coherent, beautiful even without the song.

We come too soon to the story of her death. And yet did it come too soon? A sweet life is not the sweeter for being long. Jane Austen lived years enough to fulfil her mission. She lived long enough to write six books that were masterpieces in their way—to make a world the happier for her industry.

One cannot read the story of her latter days, of her patience, her sweetness, and gratitude, without emotion. There is family trouble, we are not told of what nature. She falls ill. Her nieces find her in her dressing-gown, like an invalid, in an arm-chair in her bedroom ; but she gets up and greets them, and, pointing to seats which had been arranged for them by the fire, says : 'There is a chair for the married lady, and a little stool for you, Caroline.' But she is too weak to talk, and Cassandra takes them away.

At last they persuade her to go to Winchester, to a well-known doctor there.

'It distressed me,' she says, in one of her last, dying letters, 'to see Uncle Henry' and William Knight, who kindly attended us, riding in the rain almost the whole way. We expect a visit from them to-morrow, and hope they will stay the night; and on Thursday, which is a confirmation and a holiday, we hope to get Charles out to breakfast. We have had but one visit from *him,* poor fellow, as he is in the sick room. . . . . . God bless you, dear E.; if ever you are ill, may you be as tenderly nursed as I have been. . . .'

But nursing does not cure her, nor can the doctor save her to them all, and she sinks from day to day. To the end she is full of concern for others.

' As for my dearest sister, my tender, watchful, indefatigable nurse has not been made ill by her exertions,' she writes. 'As to what I owe her, and the anxious affection of all my beloved family on this occasion, I can only cry over it, and pray God to bless them more and more.'

One can hardly read this last sentence with dry eyes. It is her parting blessing and farewell to those she had blessed all her life by her presence and her love—that love which is beyond death; and of which the benediction remains, not only spoken in words, but by the ever-present signs and the tokens of those lifetimes which do not end for us as long as we ourselves exist.

They asked her when she was near her end if there was anything she wanted.

'Nothing but death,' she said. Those were her last words. She died on the 18th of July, 1817, and was buried in Winchester Cathedral, where she lies not unre-membered.

LONDON : PRINTED BY
SPOTTISWOODE AND CO., NEW-STREET SQUARE
AND PARLIAMENT STREET